T5-BPY-950

To My Wife

ACKNOWLEDGEMENTS

Hilary Davies
Peter & Diana Carter
William & Patricia Oxley
Professor Keith Ansell Pearson
Doctor Carol Diethe
Doctor David Owen
Profesor Babette Babich
Professor David Allison
Professor Peter Abbs
Doctor Arnab Banerji
The Royal Literary Fund
Harold Pinter
Aidan Andrew Dun
Professor Constant Mews
Father Alban McCoy
Margaret Hebblethwaite
Catherine Barker
Doctor Peter Thomas

'The Moral Stance of Poetry and Its Use to Us' and 'The Roll-Over Factor' were first published in *Acumen*. 'The Animated Dynamo' was first published in *The London Miscellany*. 'On the Aesthetics of Art in the Theology of Rowan Williams' was first published in *Scintilla*.

ROWAN WILLIAMS' THEOLOGY OF ART AND OTHER ESSAYS

Sebastian Barker

is

a Fellow of the Royal Society of Literature

Rowan Williams' Theology of Art
and Other Essays

Sebastian Barker

With a Prologue after Anselm of Canterbury
A Meditation on God

The Edwin Mellen Press
Lewiston•Queenston•Lampeter

PR
6052
.A6494
R69
2009

Library of Congress Cataloging-in-Publication Data

Barker, Sebastian.
  Rowan Williams' theology of art and other essays / by Sebastian Barker ; with a
prologue after Anselm of Canterbury : a meditation on God.
      p. cm.
  Includes bibliographical references and index.
  ISBN-13: 978-0-7734-4861-2
  ISBN-10: 0-7734-4861-6
  I. Title.

hors série.

A CIP catalog record for this book is available from the British Library.

Copyright © 2009 Sebastian Barker

All rights reserved. For information contact

The Edwin Mellen Press   The Edwin Mellen Press
Box 450   Box 67
Lewiston, New York   Queenston, Ontario
USA 14092-0450   CANADA L0S 1L0

The Edwin Mellen Press, Ltd.
Lampeter, Ceredigion, Wales
UNITED KINGDOM SA48 8LT

Printed in the United States of America

TABLE OF CONTENTS

PROLOGUE

Paraphrase of Anselm's Proof of the Existence of God[1]

An Allocution

1.   We, the monks of the monastery of Bec in Normandy, believe in, worship and love you, O God. You are, to us, something than which a greater cannot be imagined.

2.   We are aware that, in the Psalms, we have read, 'The fool hath said in his heart, There is no God.'[2] We would like to express this point of view in a different way. We would like to say, 'A good, highly intelligent man, who is no fool, has said in his heart, There is no God.'

3.   This man, who is now with us, agreed to take into his mind the idea of God as 'something than which a greater cannot be imagined.' He took this idea into his mind. He confirmed it was there. But when we asked him if he believed in the idea as a fact which existed in reality, he rejected this as unacceptable. He said he did not believe the idea in his mind had any reality in fact outside his own mind.

4.   All of us accepted that the idea of God as 'something than which a greater cannot be imagined' existed in our minds, including our friend, who was no fool. All of us also accepted that, for our friend, this something had no reality in fact outside his own mind, as it did for us.

2

5.   We said to him that this something could not exist, however, in the mind alone. This was because, we argued, if it was imagined to exist both in the mind and in reality, this was greater than if it existed in the mind alone. He looked bemused, but he agreed with us.

6.   Since this something could be imagined to exist both in the mind and in reality, our friend accepted that, in that case, it was indeed reasonable and legitimate to imagine that this was greater. He agreed that if this something was imagined to exist in reality, as well as in the mind, this was indeed greater than if it existed in the mind alone, even if it did not exist in reality in fact at all.

7.   We then pointed out to him that the idea of 'something than which a greater cannot be imagined', which *we* held in our minds, is not different from, and cannot be different from, the idea of 'something than which a greater cannot be imagined', which *he* held in his mind. This was because the ideas are identical in both cases: 'something than which a greater cannot be imagined'. That he accepted.

8.   But, we pointed out, we had already seen and agreed that that which is imagined to exist both in the mind and in reality is greater than that which is imagined to exist in the mind alone. Our friend concurred that it was therefore reasonable and legitimate to say that 'something than which a greater cannot be imagined' was more correctly imagined to exist both in the mind and in reality, even if it did not exist in reality at all, because this was greater than imagining it to exist in the mind alone.

9.   It stood to reason, then, we argued, that the likelihood of 'something than which a greater cannot be imagined', which existed as a mental idea alone, being greater than 'something than which a greater cannot be imagined', which existed

both as a mental idea and in reality, was not only improbable, it was also impossible. He accepted this.

10.   He said that such a something was indeed reasonably and legitimately imagined as existing in reality as well as in the mind, even if it did not exist in reality in fact at all.

11.   But, we pointed out, since a greater imagining of 'something than which a greater cannot be imagined' was more correctly imagined when it was imagined to exist both in reality and in the mind, it was reasonable and legitimate to say that since it was more correctly imagined in this way, we did in fact imagine it more correctly in this way, even if it did not exist in reality in fact at all.

12.   He readily agreed with that. But, we added, since we were now imagining it in this juster, more correct way, we were imagining 'something than which a greater cannot be imagined', which existed both in our minds and in reality. We imagined it did not exist in our imaginations alone, but in reality also, with the proviso that to imagine it in this way was to imagine it in a juster, more correct way than imagining it to exist in the mind alone. He agreed.

13.   But, we argued, to imagine it existed in the mind alone in such a way that it could not be imagined to exist in reality at all, was demonstrably and clearly to imagine it in such a way that a greater way of imagining it *could* be imagined. This was because there was no reason to stop us imagining it to exist both in the mind and in reality, which was greater than to imagine it to exist in the mind alone.

14.   It was, therefore, both reasonable and legitimate, we argued, to imagine that it did not exist in such an unimaginative manner in the mind alone, but in the

more imaginative manner of 'something than which a greater cannot be imagined', which existed both in the mind and in reality.

15.   Our friend said he had no alternative but to agree with this. But, we added, because we had all now imagined such a something as existing in our imaginations, we could not now imagine it *not* to exist in reality. This was because, since something which existed both in the mind and in reality was greater than something which existed in the mind alone, it was demonstrably and clearly reasonable and legitimate to say that 'something than which a greater cannot be imagined' was something which we not only imagined to exist in reality but which also could be said to exist in reality in fact. This was because if such a something was not only something which we imagined to exist in reality, but was also something which we imagined did not exist in reality in fact, but in our minds alone, then this was something which was not so great.

16.   If, however, we pointed out, such a something could be said nevertheless not to exist in reality in fact, then such a 'something than which a greater cannot be imagined', which did not exist in reality in fact, was by no means the same as 'something than which a greater cannot be imagined', which did exist in reality in fact. Which was absurd. He laughed when he agreed with that.

17.   Such an object in our imaginations, then, might be said to exist in our imaginations in such a way that it might not be said to exist in our imaginations alone. But since it might justly and correctly be said to be this greatest object in our imaginations, it stood to reason that it existed both in the mind and in reality in fact also. This was the same as saying that 'something than which a greater cannot be imagined' did in fact exist in reality.

18.   We, the monks of the monastery of Bec in Normandy, believe that you are this something, O God. Our friend informed us that, if through this line of

reasoning you could be imagined to exist in such a way that you could not be imagined not to exist, that was because you could not be justly and correctly imagined not to exist, even if you could easily be unjustly and incorrectly imagined not to exist.

19.   He said, as a consequence of this, that our proof of your existence seemed to him at bottom to depend on the just and correct use of the logic of the imagination, rather than on its unjust and incorrect use.

20.   From all this, he drew the inference that you necessarily exceeded the limits of imagination. This was because, he said, being 'something than which a greater cannot be imagined', we necessarily exhausted the greatest part of our imagination imagining the least part of yourself. As he put it, whatever we imagined we knew, or knew we imagined, about you, our imagination and knowledge of you was infinitesimally small in comparison with what we did not imagine or know about you. We accepted that. But so little, he argued, could be said to add up to nothing.

21.   As he was going, he conceded that he had been captivated by our argument but not convinced by it. He said he would turn it over in his mind as he travelled. He would put it to others to see what they thought. Thanking us for our hospitality, he departed. We went in to pray, in the name of the Father, the Son, and the Holy Spirit.

———————————————

I

On the Aesthetics of Art in the Theology of Rowan Williams

'Poetry is ontology.' This remark by the French philosopher and diplomat Jacques Maritain (1882-1973), in his essay 'The Frontiers of Poetry', is quoted by Rowan Williams in his book *Grace and Necessity: Reflections on Art and Love* (2005). The words slip into his text almost invisibly, yet they point to a subject as important as it is useful. For when we explore the words, as I will be doing, they reveal a direct connection between the practice of art and the phenomenon of being. This being, what is more, is one which is approached not so much in the *theologia gloriae*, the theology of glory, as in the *theologia crucis*, the theology of the cross. In the *theologia crucis*, the nature of being comes to us through the *via negativa* of the crucifixion and death. Williams himself has written, 'Luther asks... if they know what it is like to be in hell, because, as Luther says, only if you have been in hell can you be a theologian (a statement which I think is true and should be engraved on the portals of every theological institution in the world).'[1] There can be no doubt that Williams means what he says. So we are not talking about any kind of poetry, art, or ontology that does not start from the absolute abnegation of God in evil, catastrophe, death, and nothingness. The poetry, art and ontology under discussion here start from the Christian conception of hell. The reason why this is important, as well as useful, is because it offers an aesthetic of art which is realistic in the current age. As Williams says 'Theology begins here, with the Godless world at its most extreme.'[2]

Williams glosses 'poetry is ontology' with 'it has to do with our knowledge of being itself.'[3] Taken together, these two remarks are the key to his aesthetic. We get the best entrance to this in his book *The Wound of Knowledge*, first published in 1979 when he was 29. I had to check his age to believe it.

Allowing for the fact that the second edition of 1990 revises the first edition, the very aura, achievement, and seriousness of the book at such an age are awesome. Subtitled 'Christian Spirituality from the New Testament to St John of the Cross', the work carries the burden of three thousand years of 'profound contradictoriness'.[4] On the one hand we have the miracle of Christ. On the other we have the historical recurrence of horror. 'It is the sense of God's absence that is the pitch of the believer's agony.'[5]

In his take on 'the terrible eighty-ninth Psalm', *Job,* the Suffering Servant passages in *Isaiah, Lamentations,* 'the appalling history of Christian anti-semitism'[6] (and its origins in *The New Testament*), Paul's letters, Ignatius of Antioch, Origen and 'divine *eros*'[7] (otherwise known as the erotics of God), Basil the Great, Augustine, Cassian, Benedict, Dionysius the Pseudo-Areopagite, Bernard of Clairvaux, Aquinas, Eckhart, Luther, and John of the Cross – to name only some of his principal figures and ideas – we see how easily 'spirituality can be an escape from Christ'[8] and how 'to know forgiveness in the midst of hell because of the cross of Christ is the criterion of true Christian faith.'[9] There is a contradiction – the false and the true – at the 'heart of classical Christian spirituality'[10] and he faces it head on with fearless and penetrating energy. This is no ordinary mind coming towards us to make an aesthetic of art. It is the mind of a theologian and poet. For him, art is not a pastime, but a perpetual practice to resolve the contradiction.

He begins the construction of his aesthetic by revealing his up-to-date familiarity with the critical jargon of the verbal arts. He also notes, accurately, 'serious debate about the nature of visual and plastic art' is not a 'particularly visible feature of our intellectual life.'[11] His aim is to discover 'what the process of artistic *composition* entails and what it assumes'[12] (his italics). When he finds 'a level of embarrassment' among the aesthetic theorists he has considered, who include Geoffrey Hill in *The Lords of Limit,* Seamus Heaney in *The Redress of Poetry,* and Josef Herman on painting, it is clear in the reader's mind that for Williams this embarrassment stems from an inability to commit without quibbling to a *Christian* aesthetic[13] (my italics). As a theologian and poet with a firm grasp of the historical past, this inability strikes him as a pity. What is wrong, he implies, when poets such as Hill and Heaney, who inhabit the Christian dispensation, find Christianity an embarrassment or at best something about which to equivocate? Williams, therefore, sets out to discover what it is to compose or make a work of art in an unequivocally Christian sense. This will be neither embarrassed by nor ashamed of its theological roots, but conscious of and happy about them. Is there, he suggests, 'an unavoidably theological element to all artistic labour'?[14], to which his implicit answer is a resounding Yes!

He is alert to modernism 'as essentially that approach to art that concentrates on the fabric, inner and outer, of the work made rather than any supposed external reference, representational or theoretical.'[15] In this alertness, he is very much in the lineage of Maritain, who is himself fairly and squarely in the school of Aquinas. For Aquinas, beauty is 'id quod visum placet', that which pleases when seen. Williams comments, 'What matters is what *this* work requires; a feature may be in itself jarring or even terrible, but may still be "what pleases" in its context'[16] (his italics). This is an important point, which Williams takes care to get across, especially in his treatment of Flannery O'Connor. In the depiction of evil in a work of art, it is not appropriate that the depiction is watered down to suit a theory which applies to something other than the work of art. If in the theory of *this* work, the depiction of an absolute form of evil is required, it is to miss the point of the work to depict evil in a relative form. Each of Shakespeare's characters, good or evil or something in between, is drawn to be true to that character's genius, not to an abstract morality or a well-meaning guide to writing plays. For Aquinas and Maritain, as for Williams, 'the life of a finished work'[17] exists on three inter-exchanging levels: the integrity or inner logic of the composition; the proportions or consonance of the whole and its sense of harmony and unity with the receiver's mind; and the splendour or radiance (*splendor* or *claritas*) actively drawing in the receiver's mind.[18]

It is wise to notice in this 'the production of beauty cannot be a goal for the artist'.[19] Much more interestingly, beauty is a side-effect, an off-shoot, of what Aquinas means by *splendor formae,* splendour of form. When the three characteristics of a work of art are in place, splendour of form generates an overflow of presence, an exuberance of being. Beauty is something which comes into being in this way when these three prior requirements are interacting, *integrity, consonance, radiance*[20] (my italics).

In this light, contemporary art looks confused. It is a confusion of either beauty for beauty's sake; or 'a replacement of beauty by an appeal to a work's fidelity to the artist's *subjective* integrity'[21] (his italics). William concludes, 'Thus the great problems of contemporary art are emotionalism and intellectualism' – too much beauty for beauty's sake with the consequent disastrous reduction to the emotions aroused by this; or too much concentration on what is in the artist's mind with the consequent disastrous reduction to the intellectual points to be made about this.[22]

It is at this stage in his argument that the phrase 'poetry is ontology' occurs. By adding 'it has to do with our knowledge of being itself', Williams introduces the notion that the making of a work of art is concerned with neither beauty nor the artist's psyche but 'being itself' and our knowledge of it. There is, in short, an object to poetry and art, a purpose, an aim: being itself. When we observe that Maritain, like Aquinas, Aristotle, Heraclitus, and Parmenides before him, associates orientation towards being with intelligence, and orientation towards intelligence with being, poetry and art appear to be not so much acts of will as acts of intelligence. This is why Maritain calls art 'a virtue of the practical intellect'. It makes intelligence use of what is actually there.[23] There is, in being, substantially more, to put it mildly, than meets our eyes. Art cannot be simply imitative, because this would depict a specious surface, visual or otherwise, omitting the depth of being to which that surface is attached.

There is, however, a danger in becoming too involved in the essential reality of pure being. To do so is to commit 'the sin of the angels'.[24] Too much concern with the reality of being, working in tandem with too little concern for the world in which we live, leads to vapidity, hollowness, the work of art as a vacuous thing. There must be a clear sense of an externally given world. Maritain traces 'the sin of the angels' to the Renaissance, 'the cultural moment in which the artist becomes fully self-conscious', as Williams reports.[25] We sense 'an urgency to express the individual self without reserve'; 'perfect abstract expression'.[26] But 'the inevitable failure to allay this passion for total self-embodiment, for the "transubstantiation" of the self..., leads to blasphemy and despair.'[27] 'Mallarméan "pure poetry" leads to an aesthetic crisis.'[28] The sin of the angels.

'Art challenges the finality of appearance... not in order to destroy but to ground, amplify, fulfil. It aims at "transcendental realism"... [It] speaks to intelligence, inviting intelligence to recognize its truth... It demands... contemplation.'[29] Williams is very good at conveying the idea that art works at a level 'at which the conventional bounds between world and subject are breached'. Because poetic composition 'transgresses the ordinary bounds of conscious intellectual activity, its roots must be located in the *preconscious* life of the intellect'[30](his italics). Williams is here making himself transparent to Maritain. There is a strong hint in this of poetic composition somehow or other being in touch with the Jungian unconscious. The rhythms of the working of the Jungian unconscious, the way it acts upon our minds, the way it moulds our mental ideas 'so as to generate coherent images', the way it allows us to see 'spiritual forms',[31] suggest the pre- or unconscious life of the intellect is something to be taken 'absolutely seriously'.[32] The issue before us, therefore, is how does the artist cope with the work of the art to be made? It stands before him or her uncreated as something not yet in being. How is it to be brought into being? And what is it?

'The issue is always and only about the integrity of the work.'[33] Williams' grip on this point is a spur to any artistic conscience. Integrity cannot be bought. It is quite possible it cannot even be found. So how does an artist go about the job of art? 'The artist first listens and looks for the pulse or rhythm that is not evident.'[34] Williams derives this from Maritain's word *pulsions.* 'At the root of specifically poetic labour is what he calls a "musical stir", an intuition of something like rhythm... this "intuitive pulsion" is what is most essential to poetry.'[35] 'Modern poetry', moreover, 'pushes us back towards the deeper "pulsions" – which seem... to be something like units of imaginative sense, clusters of feeling, or even "knots" of imagery and cross-reference.'[36]

So what is going on? 'It is all to do with things "being more than they are".'[37] 'Maritain speaks of how "things are not only what they are", how they "give more than they have".'[38] From what we have seen so far, this extra quality in things, this excess or exuberance of substance which they appear to have, seems to come from their tie-up with being – from their lack of separation from being. If a thing has being, there will be no enlightened mind encircling and enclosing it – smothering it – in understanding, stamping a subjective or objective definition on it. Rather, the mind receives as much of the being of the thing as it is able. This may not be very much. So when the artist's mind dilates on the possibility of a work of art, the thing in mind, if it is to have being, is demonstrably not imprisoned by that mind, but, if anything, free to be, free to exist, according to the artist's talent. It is not an impossible jump from this to the idea that 'art necessarily relates in some way to "the sacred".'[39] What we are witnessing, therefore, in Williams' aesthetic, is the slow but sure emergence of 'a picture of divine *poiesis*'.[40]

Having established his *modus operandi*, Williams sets out in *Grace and Necessity* to tackle David Jones and Mary Flannery O'Connor. These are informed choices, because both artists were Catholics who had seen the bloody and rotten underbelly of life, but who did not flinch from their callings as artists. What David Jones saw in the First World War, for example, defies belief. Williams does not make it easy for himself by taking on these two, but it is to his credit that he did, because in the event his aesthetic not only holds up but has the more to offer for it.

'The maker's obedience is to the integrity of the thing made, to the unfolding logic in the process of making, as the work discloses itself – not to a close specification of what is *needed*[41] (his italics). For Williams, 'what is perhaps Maritain's most significant contribution' is 'his analysis of art as exposing the "excess" of the material environment ("things are more that they are").' 'Maritain's principle, so close to the heart of the modernist aesthetic, [is] that the made object is its own "world" of reference.'[42] In drawing us closer to his aims, Williams notices that the artistic superiority of David Jones over Eric Gill involves the idea that Gill 'was not a man to whom you could ascribe much in the way of "negative capability".'[43] Negative Capability is the quality John Keats identified in Shakespeare as one of his leading characteristics, 'that is when man is capable of being in uncertainties, Mysteries, doubts, without any irritable reaching after fact and reason.'[44] This is the quality which allows the maker to concentrate on the integrity, consonance, and radiance of the work, without getting bogged down in any kind of detail which does not pertain to the work.

Williams also notices the superiority of Jones over Gill in their different approaches to modernity. He cites what Jonathan Miles said of Gill, 'He side-stepped modernism.'[45] Jones, by contrast, took it on with spectacular success, to shine brightly beside James Joyce and T. S. Eliot. I would say that if *Finnegans Wake* is the *The Book of Kells* of the 20th century in verbal form, and *Four Quartets* is the poetry of a Christian Heraclitus written under the shadow of the Second World War, the works of David Jones, visual and verbal, stand with them in modernity in an equal aurole of honour. The ancient parallel with David Jones is Ezekiel. This is especially noticeable in his poem, 'A, a, a, Domine Deus', which took Jones thirty years to write (c. 1938-1966). The very title is taken from *Ezekiel* 9:8 and 11:13. Both witnessed the horrors of war first-hand yet retained belief through the eclipse of God. And both were artists of the first order. So what Williams calls in Jones a 'receptivity to sacramental theology'[46] is also to be found in Joyce and Eliot. It is how this sacramental theology works in an aesthetic of art that we must now address.

'The artwork is... an extension of "nature"; but it is so by the thoroughness of its transmutation of given nature into another material reality that reflects it and in so doing alters it and displays the hidden "more than it is".'[47] In his discussion of 'Cyfarchiad', a Jones drawing of flowers, birds, and hedge, Williams mentions the showing of the 'more than it is'. We are getting closer to 'a visual transcription of Jones's ever-deepening preoccupation with the image of the land itself as "The Sleeping Lord", the immanent and imminent presence of God's meanings, pregnant in the local and immediate.'[48] Not a slight thing to approach, or withdraw from.

Williams calls *The Anathémata* of David Jones 'a thicket of allusion'.[49] He draws our attention to how the poem develops the idea of 'the hunt in the thicket'. He is picking up on the Dominican theologian Thomas Gilby, who describes the mind as 'a hunter of forms'.[50] Williams tells us how, in the Preface, Jones 'lays out the process of searching for poetic form as a search for the complex of inter-reference that makes up the cultural identity of the poet.'[51] 'It is a hunt for what makes the poet's mind possible.' It is a hunt for 'what makes *any* poet possible'[52] (his italics). The process of searching for poetic form is the hunt for 'the ontology… of a universe that is inextricably both material and significative, where things matter intensely, but matter in ways that breach boundaries and carry significance beyond what they tangibly are.'[53] In the most delicate sense, this is the hunt for the technique of composition, for the technique of the poet as the technician of the sacred.

The hunt for the ontology of things in the sacramental theology of Williams' aesthetic of art might well be termed the hunt for *the ontotheological connection.* Jones finds this in the Catholic Mass, for this is the location in which *The Anathémata* is set.[54] Williams: 'The substance of Christ's body is such that it is real only in the matter of the world – but no less intelligibly… in the matter of the sacrament or the believing community than in the flesh that could be handled in Galilee.'[55] What are the implications of this for us? It is easy to see how the substance of Christ's body may be imagined to be both what it is in the matter of the world and what it is in the matter of the sacrament. Of Christ's body it can be said 'That flesh is more than it is, gives more than it… has,'[56] for I think most of us would agree that Christ's body conveys the splendour of form of something more theologically illuminating than an unpretentious carpenter or a corpse. Christ's body may therefore be thought of as a supreme example of Maritain's idea of a thing being more than it is. Jones sets his poem in the Mass, because it is in this setting and in this light that his technique allows him to pursue the integrity, consonance, and radiance, which he is after. Famously subtitled 'fragments of an attempted writing', the epic poem called *The Anathémata* could not really have been anything else. The Mass is assuredly not there to be enclosed by a mind. Williams is keen to have us understand 'Maritain's dictum about the incompleteness of authentic art, its woundedness by the infinite'[57] – and this is doubtless a sensible way of looking at art. *The Anathémata* will do as a good example of incompleteness, woundedness, in authentic art.

Williams observes of our times, 'the sense of ontological depth to a metaphor... has shrunk dramatically.'[58] He related this to 'the ways in which the modern imagination is radically deprived of most of what made the world of signs possible, natural and intelligible in the past.'[59] For him, Jones is a signpost pointing towards greater ontological depth to metaphor. So Jones is himself a sign. This signposting happens, of course, 'decisively and uniquely, in the life of Christ.'[60] As Jones says of Christ on the title page of his *Epoch and Artist*, following closely the Jesuit theologian Maurice de la Taille, 'He placed himself in the order of the signs.' If 'sacramental action is the supreme illumination of what and who we are, and art fails to understand itself without sacramental reference',[61] the job of art is to employ intelligence to uncover and join the order of signs through the use of sacramental reference in a made work.

This is not easy. 'The artist struggles to let the logic of what is there display itself in the particular concrete matter being worked with.'[62] Williams rephrases this eloquently, 'You have to find what you must obey, artistically.'[63] If our hunt for quarry is successful, 'Imagination produces not a self-contained mental construct but a vision that escapes control.'[64] 'The artist does not exhaust the significance of his or her labour, but creates an object, a schema of perceptible data, that will have about it the same excess as the phenomena that stimulated the production in the first place.'[65] 'Observing the integrity of what is made is the mode of the artist's love.'[66] So the quarry is captured, even as it escapes control, in the quality of the talent of the artist's love.

At this concluding stage, it is necessary to emphasise a particular and peculiar point. This concerns not our approach to, but our withdrawal from, being. 'The artist doing his job *withdraws* in the process of making so that [the] complex interaction of presences can occur'[67] (my italics). This remark by Williams is pure Heidegger (1889-1976). Why? Because Heidegger realised that even the slightest glimpse of being reveals rather more than we can take in. In other words, the slightest glimpse of being necessitates withdrawal from it to form any notion of it whatsoever.[68] He also applied this idea to the making of a work of art. The withdrawal from it is as important as the approach to it. For the same reason: the being of the work of art.

Since Christ is indeed hung in the order of signs, we can say that it is through Christ crucified, the *theologia crucis*, that we can form some sort of realistic idea of being as such, because this can be channelled to us through Christ's being on the cross. The work of art is therefore that portion of being which the artist translates from a vision of it, with the help and mediation of the Christian system of belief. 'Without art we should not fully see what *sanctity* is about'[69] (his italics). In this context, the integrity, consonance, and radiance in a work, its sanctity, 'is the work of love',[70] the secret, hidden work of the artist. 'It would be very eccentric to see art as central to the distinctively human and at the same time as operating independently of love.'[71]

The work of love, it stands to reason, is work never to be undertaken lightly but in full knowledge of the hurt it may bring down on itself.[72] But without the work of love we do not fully connect with our being in the world, its art and its sanctity. So the work of love is the work of poetry, the work of art. All three are ontological: they have to do with our knowledge of being itself. For without grounding in the *mysterium tremendum et fascinans*, love, poetry, and art have no object, no purpose, no aim, and the works of love, of poetry, of art, are as redundant as the functioning of things, of worlds, with no soul in them. '*Being is the transcendens pure and simple*'[73] – always seen through the dark glass of the actual world in which we live.

The aesthetics of art developed by Rowan Williams, in his responsible theological position, is important and useful, therefore, because it shows us how to be reverential as well as realistic in our artistic work in the 21st Century.

_____

II

The Moral Stance of Poetry and Its Use to Us

> At all events we are well aware that poetry being
> such as we have described it, is not to be regarded
> seriously as attaining to the truth.

Plato, *The Republic*[1]

This is the heart of the matter. Poetry *being such as Plato has described it* is not to be regarded seriously as attaining to the truth. But has Plato described poetry as it is or as he imagines it to be?

Let me apply my understanding of Plato's theory of ideas to this question.

Just as, in reality, God, or the idea of the Good, makes only one chair or table, which is to say God makes the idea of chair or table; so God makes only one poetry, which is to say God makes the idea of poetry. Now, just as carpenters make many chairs and tables, but can never be said to make a real chair or table, because these can only be made by God; so poets make many poems, but can never be said to make a real poem, because this can only be made by God. In this way, just as carpenters make only good, mediocre, or bad chairs and tables, so poets make only good, mediocre, or bad poems – the good ones in both cases approaching closer to the God-made originals.

So, to consider poetry at all, just as to consider a chair or a table at all, we have to imagine the original made by God. It stands to reason, therefore, that we have to imagine God's poetry in reality first, before we can have any idea of what poetry might be in the human sphere. This is because the reality is God's and the simulacrum man's. Once we have some grasp of God's idea of poetry, we can proceed to compare the poetries of men and women with it, just as we consider other works such as chairs and tables with their divine originals. The idea of poetry with which we furnish ourselves when we contemplate God's poetry leads us to ask this question: What is the idea of God's poetry in reality?

As Plato imagines it, if my understanding of his theory of ideas is to remain consistent, the idea of God's poetry in reality must be the reality of poetry. But this is in flat contradiction of Plato's demonstrable statement that 'poetry being such as we have described it, is not to be regarded seriously as attaining to the truth.'

How has such an apparent contradiction come about? Why, in fact, is it that Plato has such an awry opinion of poetry and poets? What is the moral stance of poetry that it so upset this giant among moral philosophers? It seems from *The Republic* that the moral stance of poetry, whatever that might be, hits at the heart of Plato's idea of just and responsible government. Is it possible that this is true? If it is, doesn't it suggest poetry is something very odd indeed?

If we go back to the beginning of *The Republic*, for I have quoted from Book Ten, we can pick up on Socrates making it clear that to hear injustice praised and do nothing about it is an impiety. We get the feeling he is a sound defender of what is holy. Plato makes Socrates, if we like, a semiotic of the holy life. The company he graces with his presence is palpably involved in the discussion of the theoretical founding of the just State. The vital point he makes is that young minds growing up in such a State must not be told stories which are not true. Socrates says:

> Now the founders of a State ought to know the general forms in which poets should cast their tales, but to make the tales is not their business.[2]

What poets do when they cast their tales is of the utmost importance to the founders of the State because it involves the teaching of the young at an impressionable age when ideas are irrevocably formed.

If truth is misrepresented in poets' tales, the consequences are disastrous for the State. What such conceivable misrepresentations boil down to is the misrepresentation of God or the Good. Here is Socrates:

> God is always to be represented as he truly is, whatever be the sort of poetry, epic, lyric, or tragic, in which the representation is given.[3]

Socrates is addressing Adeimantus, singer of oracles. He suggests that God is 'truly good', 'hurts not', 'does no evil', cannot be 'a cause of evil', is 'advantageous', is 'the cause of well-being', and is not the cause of 'all things, but of the good only.'

> For few are the goods of human life, and many are the evils, and the good is to be attributed to God alone; of the evils the causes are to be sought elsewhere, and not in him.[4]

God, like Apollo, is all lightness and brightness. There is nothing dark, terrible, or evil about him. This point is absolutely crucial for poets to understand, because on it Plato hangs Socrates's right to determine 'the general forms in which poets should cast their tales'. Adeimantus agrees with Socrates that God is not the author of all things but only of the good. Socrates goes on:

> Then we must not listen to Homer or to any other poet who is guilty of saying that two casks lie at the threshold of Zeus, full of lots, one of good, the other of evil lots.[5] (Cf. Homer, *The Iliad*, XXIV, 527)

Plato through the voice of Socrates rams the point home. He is an aboriginal moralist of the strongest stripe. His words repay the closest scrutiny:

> And if a poet writes of suffering, or on any similar theme, either we must not permit him to say that these are works of God, or if they are of God, he must devise some sort of explanation of them such as we are seeking; he must say that God did what was just and right, and they were the better for being punished; but that those who are punished are miserable, and that

God is the author of their misery – the poet is not to be permitted to say. That God being good is the author of evil to anyone is to be strenuously denied. Such a fiction is suicidal, ruinous, impious.[6]

The founders of the State, in other words, must prescribe for themselves control of religion, control of the imaginative forces behind it, control of theology in short. This above all: the founders of the State must control theology. Or as we might put it today, ideology.

Plato is adamant that to allow poets to tell tales which are not true is impious, ruinous, suicidal to the State. Poets must toe the moral line both during the creation and throughout the duration of the State. They must not devote their powers to what would amount to ideological corruption of the young. He will not permit the powers of poetry, in its influence over the formative stages of the mind, serve an evil end.

There are weighty matters at stake here. Plato, at this turn of his argument, is attempting to show that justice is in every way a superior approach to life than injustice. Justice, and the framing of laws to uphold it, is a good idea, all agree, to protect man from man's nature. Clearly, if poets pollute or pervert the idea that God is good and just, and promote the idea that God is the source and the author of evil and injustice, then the foundations of the State will be on hopelessly unstable grounds. It is for this reason, therefore, that poets unable to toe his moral line are banned from Plato's Republic.

This is an interesting point in relation to the fate of Salman Rushdie and his book *The Satanic Verses* (1988). There was a critical point in the life of Muhammad (*c.* 570-632 AD) when some of the revelations he had been receiving, and which had been proclaimed in public, were cancelled and others substituted in their place. These are the original 'satanic verses'. As W. Montgommery Watt has it in *Muhammad: Prophet and Statesman*: 'The explanation given for the change was that Satan had managed to slip in the false verses of the first version without Muhammad noticing it.'[7] His cautious conclusion about this 'strange and surprising story', in which so much is historically unsure, and in which 'the prophet of the most uncompromisingly monotheistic religion seems to be authorising polytheism', is that 'it seems certain that Muhammad recited the "satanic verses" as part of the Qur'ān and later recited another revelation abrogating them.'[8]

We know that 'throughout his career Muhammad was specially sensitive to intellectual or literary attacks... They were for him an unforgivable sin.'[9] Just how unforgivable we learn when we see the fate of two of his prisoners not released in the customary way for ransom money. He had them executed. 'One had written verses about him, and the other had said that his own stories about things Persian were as good as the tales of the Qur'ān.'[10]

Why is it so important to Muhammad to abrogate the 'satanic verses' and to be perhaps just a touch ungentle when it comes to literary criticism? It is impossible to overstate, I believe, the importance to both Plato and the Republic and Muhammad and Islam that God is good and just and is in no way the source and author of evil. If this fundamental axiom is called into question in any way, especially along the lines that God is indeed the source and author of evil, the threat to security must be seen as absolute. The slightest hint that evil, injustice, or any satanic deception emanates from the Godhead must be crushed immediately.

So when Salman Rushdie raised the spectre of polytheism by publishing *The Satanic Verses,* and gave rise, therefore, to the possibility of thinking of the Godhead as evil, unjust, and satanic, he had to be crushed immediately through the proclamation of the *fatwa.* The issue of the moral stance of poetry leads a poet to this point. The choice is clear. Do I toe the moral line of the state? Or do I follow the moral line of my muse?

The resolution of such a crisis hangs on a simple point. Is God in fact good and just, or is God also evil, unjust, and satanic? We may well ask, how can we be sure of anything about God? How can we be sure of anything about morality? Isn't it easier and wiser to settle for secular relativism and be done with these questions?

A true poet with a true calling, however, is not someone, I would suggest, who will dismiss these questions with impunity. It is false theology, false mythology, false ideology, false poetry, false poets, that Plato rejects in *The Republic.* Not poets as such.[11] This is an emphasis too easily overlooked by poets unsure of philosophers in general and Plato in particular. Plato makes it crystal clear it is not poets as such who arouse the philosophers' need to ban them from the Republic, but the unholy doctrines they might adopt, consciously or unconsciously. This is a pressing matter for Plato because the poets are apparently subject to demonic possession as well as an inability to reveal to rational understanding the sources of their inspiration.

Plato has a particular eye on the tragic poet:

> We shall be right in refusing to admit him into a well-ordered State, because he awakens and nourishes and strengthens the feelings and impairs the reason... And the same may be said of lust and anger and all the other affections, of desire and pain and pleasure... in all of them poetry feeds and waters passions instead of drying them up; she lets them rule, although they ought to be controlled.[12]

Poetry, as Plato understands it, may undermine the State. 'Of the many excellences which I perceive in the order of our State, there is none which upon reflection pleases me better than the rule about poetry.'[13]

> Hymns to the gods and praises of famous men are the only poetry which ought to be admitted into our State. For if you go beyond this and allow the honeyed muse to enter, either in epic or lyric verse, not law and the reason of mankind, but pleasure and pain will be the rulers in our State.[14]

'There is,' Plato tells us, 'an ancient quarrel between philosophy and poetry.'[15] He has no doubt which has the upper hand in this. 'If she [poetry] will only prove her title to exist in a well-ordered State, we shall be delighted to receive her – we are very conscious of her charms; but we may not on that account betray the truth.'[16] In summary then, Plato welcomes poetry, if only an adequate defence of it can be found. As matters stand at the end of *The Republic*, Homer and the tragedians, not to mention the comedians, are out. So how may the moral stance of the just State and the moral stance of poetry be squared?

The incorporation of evil, injustice, and the satanic into the Godhead is ruled out in traditional Platonic metaphysics, in traditional Christian metaphysics, and, as we have seen, in traditional Islamic metaphysics. God cannot be both good and evil. Such a view is not only illogical but profoundly offensive to a believer. Does the metaphysics of poetry, traditional, modern, post-modern, or otherwise, work in the ways these philosophical and religious traditions do? Or does it possess an altogether different *modus operandi*?

Few poets address these questions with anything like the degree of seriousness they deserve. This may be because their positions in society are secure, central, and above board, in which case the thought of the work involved is uncomfortable, and may even call their positions into question. Or because their positions in society are insecure, marginal, and underground, in which case the thought of the work involved is off-putting and might get them nowhere, or even worsen their positions. How poetry incorporates evil, injustice, and the satanic into the Godhead, without violating a good and just hair on that head, remains for one or two others, however, wherever placed in society, a vocational compulsion.

It must be said at once that this is not to invoke polytheism or any other ism from the history of philosophy and religion in the west. It is to lay bare the metaphysics by which poetry has operated since the time of Thespis and Aeschylus; and indeed for much longer than that. Here is the model in which the metaphysics may be seen.

We imagine the cosmos compressed into a sphere about the size of a football. We imagine the life force pulsing outwards from the centre of the ball. When the life force hits the surface of the ball in a continual sequence of pulsations, all the phenomena we behold in existence shape the surface in a continual sequence of change. We observe these surface phenomena rise and fall, ripple and fade, seethe and settle, not unlike the waves on the surface of the oceans. We see good and evil events, just and unjust acts, all part of the phenomenon of the sphere turning before our eyes. We turn to each other and say, 'Who are we imagining this?'

We recognise our common humanity and do not for a moment mistake ourselves for gods. We ask ourselves the question most deeply troubling us. Are we to imagine Plato's idea of the Good, the Christian God, the Muhammadan Allah, and the Buddhist Nirvana – to name only a few -- as part of, or as the whole of, this sphere? Are they part of, or the whole of, the cosmos and the phenomena beheld in it? Or are they part of, or the whole of, an extra-cosmic noumenon, being, imagining us imagining our model? Are they enclosed by the sphere, where we have imagined good and evil, justice and injustice, so that they might be thought of as the sources and authors of evil, injustice, and the satanic? Or are they bigger than our model, our imaginations, and ourselves?

Is it possible, therefore, that quarrelling with neither philosophy nor religion, our inference of such an extra-cosmic noumenon accords with an idea of the Godhead which does not participate in our model? This means, *a fortiori*, that our idea of the Godhead, as something external to our model and ourselves, is also external to all our apprehensions of good and evil, justice and injustice, the angelic and the satanic, and all the other various phenomena of the cosmos.

The Godhead, as Godhead, incorporates both ourselves and our model into itself, without in any way being affected by what is in us or in our model. God and the poetry of God are unidentifiable with any of the phenomena in ourselves or in our model. God and the poetry of God are therefore unidentifiable with good and evil, justice or injustice, the angelic or the satanic, or with anything else. This is because moral matters, like neutral phenomena, are parts of a whole greater than themselves. God and the poetry of God are the whole of the case, of which moral matters and natural phenomena are parts. Human intellection as such is another part.

Poetry, therefore, serves the just State, and is without limitation useful to it, because it is, in this representation, defined as the intermediary between divine power and human cognition. Poetry at its most useful, therefore, has the moral stance of the prophet: the poet as avatar or founder of the just State. Poetry at its most useless has the moral stance of the egotist: the poet as adventurer in the little world of me. In between these two extremes we find poetry of greater or lesser usefulness: the poet as tragedian, comedian, or historian. To a greater or lesser extent, therefore, the poet intercedes between the divine power of God and the finite power of man. When we say, 'Thy will be done on earth, as it is in heaven', we acknowledge the efficacy of the poet in each of us.

III

The Roll-Over Factor

The literary world sees from time to time the roll-over factor. This is a natural phenomenon brought on by a continual emergence of a younger generation, a continual moving on of a maturer generation, and a continual dying of an older generation. Caught up in the roll-over factor, and the heart of it, is the existence of literary merit. What is literary merit? Ah, but that is what the roll-over factor is all about.

If no one aspires to write literature, there is no roll-over factor. But if people do, and their number is legion, we are all on board, rolling over each other, no more able to stop the phenomenon than we are to stop the galaxy revolving.

I first became conscious of the roll-over factor at twelve. My mother had a large library of books; a strange portion of this consisted of literary magazines, notably the so-called 'small magazines', the traditional breeding grounds of talent. But she had not just the up-to-date ones, but those going back five or six decades. I was spellbound by the names on the covers of these magazines. I could see people rising up, becoming prominent, and fading away again. There was something magical about the phenomenon, this aspiration towards an imaginary heaven.

I was to notice that success, money, and fame in literature do not necessarily bring any lessening of the effort needed to reach such a heaven. As we see in T. S. Eliot, such outward achievements may well mask personal failure, poverty of spirit, and obscurity of inner identity. As his biographer Lyndall Gordon has pointed out, 'He is a man who has striven for success to conceal from himself a deeper failure.'[1] Eliot's second marriage late in life was to change all that, but the truth of it for much of his time cannot be brushed aside. What twelve-year-old wants to aspire to an outward success which for the most part masks an inner failure?

There must be a purpose, something to aim for, beyond recognition by the world at large. If understanding of this is lost in society, success, money, and worldly position easily usurp the purpose. The rat-race within the roll-over factor takes over. It is greatly to Eliot's credit that he kept on searching for the purpose. Nothing, in truth, kept it from him. Success or failure in literature may be taken to mean, then, success or failure at *something beyond recognition.*

Since we know well enough what 'recognition' and 'beyond' mean, we are down to one word 'something' to understand this definition. A 'thing' is derived from the Common Teutonic and Old English for 'a meeting, an assembly, a deliberative or judicial assembly'. In time it came to mean 'a matter brought before a court of law, a suit or case pleaded before a court'. Later, 'that with which one is concerned in action, speech, or thought'. This is the more abstract meaning. The more concrete meaning is better known: 'an entity of any kind, that which has separate or individual existence'. If we take literature as a 'thing' in both these senses, the real thing in literature is an assembly of people in which the word is made concrete.

This might take the form of a gathering of people listening to a poet reciting from a newly printed book of poems. Or it might take the form of an auditorium of people listening to a novelist bringing a novel to life. Or again it might be a comedy in full flight in a theatre. The interesting point in any given example is surely that there has to be a number of people involved in the concretion of the word. Literature may be made in a solitary head, but it takes on its proper existence only when two or three or more people are gathered together and experience it.

This is where the question of literary merit becomes most teasing. If the would-be literature does not communicate with the two or three or more people, it has no literary merit to those people. Since another audience might feel differently, a true author must embark on what we know may be a long and perilous journey in search of his or her properly appreciative audience. Success or failure is now seen to depend on two quite different things. The first is that the author does in fact have something to say. The second is that the audience does in fact exist which appreciates this. There can, of course, be no guarantee that the two pre-requisites will coincide in any given life.

The explanation of literary cliques, then, is not simply that like minds get together to indulge in a bit of *participation mystique*. The more interesting explanation is that people congregate in literary audience to experience the word made concrete. This remark suggests a deliberate allusion to the word or logos of Saint John: 'In the beginning was the Word, and the Word was with God, and the Word was God.'[2] However, there is no need to limit our consideration here to Christianity. My point is that the purpose of literature has been anciently understood to be sacred not secular.

A national literature which erases the distinction between the sacred and the secular is dangerous. Since the bulk of the literature coming at us today blurs this distinction, we are, spiritually speaking, living in dangerous times. We might notice, too, that as soon as a person becomes conscious of, and enters into, the rat-race in the roll-over factor, the law of survival of the fittest takes over. This justifies any behaviour, however mendacious, which is a disastrous state of affairs. How might we teach a nobler path along which to conduct ourselves justly in the search for sacred purpose?

By remembering the past. The state of the theatre in London gives some example of how much has been forgotten about the past. We do not, for instance, see any newly-written tragedies in the Greek or Shakespearean class appearing before our eyes. If this is a question of the lack of authorial talent, it is also a question of the lack of understanding of the ancient purpose of tragedy. The same might be said to hold true across the board in the other arts. To ask the question, what is the purpose of art? is to beg the question, what was the ancient purpose of art? But how, it might be objected, can we remember the past, if we have forgotten it? Fair point. If we are biased towards the view that art is about entertainment, this might be because entertainment is one part of it which is a pleasure to remember. Yet its most vital purpose in ancient times was not simply to give pleasure, but to cure spiritual wounds, especially those of the collected assembly or nation. It would seem recalling how to do that is not such a pleasure to remember.

In England today, we scarcely have a concept of what a spiritual wound might be, let alone how to cure one. What is more, feeling the reality of this in any artistic, social, or political context constitutes another spiritual wound in itself. The trivialisation of art in the exhibits of Damien Hirst, for example, reveals how far the contemporary art world has deviated from any ancient understanding of its purpose. Damien Hirst does not cure spiritual wounds, he causes them. Those who participate in such affliction of our spirits through the purchase of such exhibits do not well understand how a fool and his money are soon parted.

We can assert that literary or artistic merit exists at the heart of the roll-over factor, because of the abundant evidence for this on the historical record. What we need to know, nevertheless, is how to achieve and recognise such merit to bring it to life in our midst. This is not simply a question of studying or copying the historical models, but of understanding how they were made in the first place and what their original purpose was.

This might be summed up in a single phrase: overcoming the sense of depression inherent in any realistic view of life. The past, especially in the dramatic art of tragedy, teaches us that this is done by making works which mirror back to us all our activities, the good, the bad, and the evil.

This means the complete artistic truth about us does not omit anything which we might be tempted to overlook. Artistic merit, in short, is distinguished in the first instance by authorial licence to edit out nothing from human experience. All other considerations aside, this will take more than courage: understanding how it is done, if in fact it can be done at all, is clearly the most important thing for an artist. Given what happened in the 20th century alone, and given the past masters to guide and assist us, true artistic or literary merit resides, then, in the ability to cause a sufficient reaction in an audience to cure spiritual wounds. True success or failure becomes the relative success or failure of our achievement at the heart of the roll-over factor, the *something beyond recognition.*

IV

The Animated Dynamo

Henry Adams (1838-1918) teaches us something it would be unwise to ignore. This is his Venus/Virgin/Dynamo 'triangulation', which he locates at the centre of his model of history.[1] At the core of this is a vision of the physical universe.

Why is this important? What does triangulation mean? Do the Venus, the Virgin, and the Dynamo have comprehensible connotations? What kind of sense is he trying to imply by bringing them together? Why does he place their triangulation at the centre of a model of history? It will be the aim of this chapter to address these questions.

'"Triangulation: any trigonometric operation for finding a position or location by means of bearings from two fixed points a known distance apart." Thus runs one dictionary's definition of the latest Washington buzzword.' Triangulation here describes President Clinton's re-election strategy: 'It means keeping a distance from both Republicans and Democrats in Congress, and defining himself with reference to those two distinct points.'[2] The type of triangulation Adams had in mind a century before was also derived from a similar trigonometrical usage connected to surveying. But his triangulation reaches beyond surveying or American politics to a visionary model of the cosmos.

For Adams the word triangulation is important in the sense that the trinity is important in Christian theology. Both terms are triangular undertakings to give a face to a fundamental energy. To triangulate in the Adams sense is to make a triangular connection between the sexual nature of the Venus, the spiritual nature of the Virgin, and the mathematically precise physical nature of the Dynamo, insofar as all three may be said to be expressions of that fundamental energy.

The three terms Venus, Virgin, and Dynamo are to be thought of as symbolic aspects of nature. The sexual and the spiritual forces are the 'two fixed points a known distance apart'. The 'triangulation' or 'trigonometric operation' takes its bearings from our historical knowledge of them as forces to locate the third point, which is the position of the Dynamo. In other words, sex and spirit are triangulated to locate our historical knowledge of the physical nature of the cosmos.

All three points in the triangulation stand in geometrically precise relations to each other. The significance of Adam's idea, placed at the centre of a model of history, is that it implies the generation of time from the dynamics of the triangle. Sexual, spiritual, and physical forces are conceived in a tripartite form, each very much distinct yet inseparable from the others. Time arises like a miracle, as it were, out of their co-operation. By contrast, the modern scientific model of time implies its generation from the physical arm of this triangle alone.

George Smoot's view in *Wrinkles in Time* gives an honourable picture of the modern scientific model.[3] Smoot and his huge team of scientists sent a satellite called the Cosmos Background Explorer, or COBE for short, into the heavens. They wanted to detect and measure the cosmic background radiation predicted by the Big Bang theory. If they found such radiation on the required scale, this was serious additional proof of the theory of the Big Bang. If they didn't, the theory was in trouble. COBE's sensitivity turned out to be legendary. The radiation was detected and measured to the best of modern ability: not perfectly, but enough to give the theory an immense boost and front-page coverage around the world.

Smoot admitted that 'the origin of space-time remains in terra incognita',[4] but he also announced proudly that his team 'had observed the oldest and largest structures ever seen in the... universe.'[5] Here was how he described the wonders. (Referring to the images of the structures in the heavens, as they appeared on the map of the heavens on his detecting screen, he called them 'wrinkles'). 'The pattern of wrinkles I saw on the map was primordial – I knew it in my bones.

Some of the structures represented by the wrinkles were so large that they could only have been generated at the birth of the universe, not later on. I was staring at primordial wrinkles in time, the imprint of creation and the seeds of the modern universe.'[6]

The situation at work here was prefigured in the headlines of *The New York Times* for November 23rd 1951: 'POPE SAYS UNIVERSE WAS CREATED BY GOD 5 TO 10 BILLION YEARS AGO'. This was Pope Pius XII, who was taking his cue from his chief scientific adviser E. T. Whittaker.[7] Even if with Smoot and his team we were more than forty years on from this, the major difference was simply that the universe was now thought to be older. It was now thought to be over 15 billion years old. So, if we travel back in time to the beginning of any conceivable cosmological record for time, we begin to approach the start of time roughly 15 billion years ago.

It is important to realise that there is no space or time or space-time before the Big Bang: space and time were created 15 billion years ago. Therefore, just as it is implicit in archaeology and palaeontology that the past is 'made present', if only we can find it on the fossil or geological records, it is also implicit in cosmology and its theory of the Big Bang that the past is 'made present', if only we can find it on the cosmological record. We cannot scan the cosmological record except within a time period of 15 billion years, because this time period prescribes the limit of the record. We cannot, therefore, use cosmology to understand time outside the boundary of the cosmological record. Our understanding of the genesis of time, if time originates outside the purview of the cosmological record, remains, therefore, by definition, outside the purview of this particular scientific approach. This is a point to which we will return.

Taking up the lead of Pope Pius XII and his adviser, but updating it, let us imagine, for the sake of convenience, that the universe of space and time was created by God, along the lines of the Big Bang theory, 15 billion years ago. The first things of importance to emerge out of space-time in the early periods of the cosmological record were huge structures of radiation. These are the structures of radiation shown to us by the COBE satellite. In later periods, matter emerged out of these structures of radiation. So, for quite a long time after God made the Big Bang, there was no matter, only space-time and radiation? Exactly.

All this is relevant to our theme because it shows us how modern science conceives of our origins: since the radiation mapped by COBE was the dominant reality for so long after the Big Bang, and since matter did not come into its own until so much later after the Big Bang, it therefore seems inappropriate to think of a sexual Venus or a spiritual Virgin before the time that matter came into being, if we conceive of the Venus and the Virgin in material forms. Because the mathematical physics of the cosmologists holds primacy over our conception of our origins, it alone is thought to face the facts of the early seconds, minutes, and years of the cosmos, as we observe these on the cosmological record. It is, in fact, 1 to 5 billion years after the Big Bang that we come across the creation of hydrogen and helium atoms. Spiral galaxies come much later. In all seriousness, is there any likelihood of sexuality or spirituality coming into being before there are any atoms or galaxies through which they might come into being? Such in essence is the scientific argument for retaining the mathematical physics of the cosmologists in its primacy over our thinking. If the argument does not so much prove as assert its right to primacy, the possibility of the wrongness of this is also possible in time.

The way we have presented matters so far deliberately places a Catholic Pope pleading the case for God at the heart of the story. This is because we counter-assert that the cosmos predicated by the Big Bang theory of the cosmologists is not the radiant natural substance of Aristotle, which predicates the living God,[8] but belongs to an Aristotelian category somewhat less primordial than this.[9] In our account the primary predicate is God. God creates the Big Bang, the radiation, the universe of space, time, and matter, and all that issues from them. It is not the cosmologists and their Big Bang theory who create these things. Our account makes God the one true predicate of being. Any analogous reality proclaimed by the cosmologists, such as the indisputable physical reality of the cosmos in the Big Bang theory, is a subsequent or consequent predicate in our account of being. But, counters the cosmologist, what if God is not the one true predicate of being, but a supreme fiction?

This is the point where fact and fiction declare war in the bid for intellectual supremacy. Which is the superior mode of conception, the factual or the fictional? For a mind as delicate, penetrating, and persistent as Henry Adams', there could be no doubt about this. To conceive in terms of facts alone was, for him, barbaric in its indelicacy. And nor was reasoning itself, to such a mind, any more than a useful tool. We can see the drift of Adams' thought, in regard to these two points, in the following remark: 'The mind resorts to reasoning for want of training.'[10] And, as he so drolly put it, 'Adams had never met a perfectly trained mind.'[11]

Concrete facts, reasoning: these are the nursery slopes on the route towards perfect training. For Adams, a perfectly trained mind would be able to read such a thing as the supreme fiction of God and tell us how the universe of space and time, reasoning and concrete facts, came into being. Reasoning and concrete facts will clearly become important once the supreme fiction gets underway. But they can never visualise beyond themselves. We reason about concrete facts which have become concrete facts about which we can reason. This is the very world of fact. To account for it, no fact or reason is sufficient. This is because all are enclosed in that world. To account for it, we resort to fiction. Lack of imagination is just as disastrous in a scientist as in an artist. As William Blake said, 'What is now proved was once only imagined.'[12] This is the very world of fiction; the very world of imagination.

As Adams brooded on the physical reality of the cosmos, he realised his putative theory of history would have to include it: 'A historical formula that should satisfy the conditions of the stellar universe weighed heavily on his mind.'[13] Would the facts of the stellar universe, as portrayed by the cosmologists of the 21st century, have provided him with that satisfaction? Almost certainly not. This is because the formula put forward by the cosmologists, for all its subtlety, is too limited in its imaginative grasp to satisfy such a man.

In the Adams model, we do not understand fundamental energy correctly if we limit it to what is identifiable cosmologically. The sexual and the spiritual are not to be excluded from it, simply because cosmological thinking about it precludes them. After all, cosmological thinking is presently bounded by a circumference of 15 billion years. The potency of the suggestion of what existed before the first moment is unignorable, even if it is necessarily unscientific, because time is said by the scientists to be created in the Big Bang. Do models of sexual or spiritual potency have any relevance here? Must we limit ourselves to a model of physical potency alone? And what might we imagine if we combined all three models of potency?

We have often heard of sexuality and spirituality acting in unison, but mathematically precise physicality acting in unison with them as well strikes a note of originality. This was somewhat revolutionary in the late 19th century ambassadorial circles in which Adams moved. This helps to explain the mere 100 copies of his autobiographical masterpiece on its first appearance in 1907. If David Jones (1895-1974) emphasised 'the Break' between the old world view prevailing towards the middle of the 19th century and his own time, 'at the turn of a civilization' as he styled it,[14] Henry Adams' model makes a seriously impressive bid to bridge this break. The model warrants our scrutiny all the more in that a mind of David Jones's calibre was unable to conceive of such a thing, which of its own nature takes in a scientific view of the world.

If examined in more detail, the Adams model anticipates not only nuclear power and consciousness studies but a bold and enlightened attitude to sex uncommon in the social arena in any era.[15] [16] Indeed, because of this, his way of interpreting history reached over his time into the 21st century.

Adams was scrupulous and illuminating in dealing with the revelations and non-revelations to be found in faith or the lack of it. He could be said to be in this sense an arch-witness of his time and a fore-runner of our own. While he spoke of his own 'aching consciousness of religious void',[17] for example, he also made it clear he understood the 'metaphysical' dimension in the discovery of radium.[18] Such discoveries in science, which he followed so avidly, revealed 'his historical neck broken by the sudden irruption of forces totally new.'[19] His new model of history, to restore his historical neck, was the result.

As a man and above all, Henry Adams wanted 'consideration' from the United States.[20] His great-grandfather, John Adams, and his grandfather, John Quincy Adams, were both Presidents of the United States. His father, Charles Francis Adams, was minister to England during the American Civil War: he has been reliably described as one of the ablest diplomats America has produced.

Henry Adams accompanied his father during that time. Later, he was for some years Assistant Professor of History at Harvard. With such a background, the kind of consideration he wanted was necessarily of the highest order. He may well receive more in the end than he bargained for.

His more surprising points anticipating nuclear power, consciousness studies, and sexual enlightenment, for example, were made by 1900, five years before Einstein shook the world. Paul Davies in *About Time* put his finger on what it was about Einstein which made him so revolutionary: 'In 1905, Einstein plucked time from philosophy and placed it at the heart of physics. It suddenly became a physical thing, subject to laws and equations, and inviting experimental investigation.'[21] Adams cannot possibly be said to have been revolutionary in anything like the way Einstein was. His way of plucking time from philosophy and meditating about the meaning of history was closer to the humanities than the sciences. But since the Adams model targets mathematical physics in its basic triangulation, whereas Einstein can scarcely be accused of targeting sex or spirit in his theory of relativity, could it be that Adams has something to teach us about the nature of physics which Einstein does not have to teach us about the nature of sex or spirituality?

What is more, Adams spoke to us in a narrative English so elegant in its artistry and so attentive to its scientific accuracy as to make him a rare spirit on any library shelf. He is that unique gift to the reader, a historian who writes like a novelist and an autobiographer who writes like a historian.

The Venus he re-introduced, in making his triangulation, wears neither fig-leaves nor clothing to hide her sex in any way. She is as naked and as potent a Sex-Goddess as could be imagined. When he spoke of 'the power of sex' in the context of American culture, he excepted Bret Harte and Walt Whitman: 'All the rest had used sex for sentiment, never for force... American art, like the American language and American education, was as far as possible sexless.'[22] He lamented this situation, issuing a challenge to American artists inadequately met to this day. 'The Woman had once been supreme... not merely as a sentiment, but as a force. Why was she unknown in America? For evidently America was ashamed of her, and she was ashamed of herself, otherwise they would not have strewn fig-leaves so profusely all over her. When she was a true force, she was ignorant of fig-leaves, but the monthly-magazine-made American female had not a feature that would have been recognized by Adam.'[23] Let us not get side-tracked by beauty. He is talking about fundamental forces. 'Neither Diana of the Ephesians nor any of the Oriental goddesses was worshipped for her beauty. She was goddess because of her force; she was *the animated dynamo*' [24](my italics).

'An American Venus', he said, 'would never dare exist.'[25] This was because 'anyone brought up among Puritans knew that sex was sin.'[26] To Adams, 'sex was strength.'[27] The Sex-Goddess had nothing to do with sin. That view was an historical anomaly. The Sex-Goddess was strength. She was a force to be reckoned with.

His treatment of the Virgin was equally radical. 'The force of the Virgin was still felt at Lourdes, and seemed to be as potent as X-rays.'[28] In considering the Cathedral of Notre Dame of Amiens and the other great Cathedrals, he saw the Virgin as 'the force that created [them] all.'[29] His overall assessment of the power of the Virgin was uncompromising: 'Symbol or energy, the Virgin had acted as the greatest force the Western world ever felt, and had drawn man's activities to herself more strongly than any other power, natural or supernatural, had ever done; the historian's business was to follow the track of the energy.'[30]

Casting his eye over European history, Adams noticed that the Venus of Lucretius had much in common with the Virgin of Dante: 'The Venus of Epicurean philosophy survived in the Virgin of the Schools.'[31] By juxtaposing quotations, he showed that Lucretius invoking the Venus revealed just how similar his Venus was to the Virgin invoked by Dante. Unfortunately, 'all this was to American thought as though it had never existed.'[32] For just as an American Venus would never dare exist, so 'an American Virgin would never dare command.'[33] By 1895, he told us, 'he [had] begun to feel the Virgin [and the] Venus as force.'[34] Naturally enough, both had different historical track-records; but, as the quotations indicated, there was a metamorphic relation between them.

For those concerned with gender politics, it is evident that if we supplant the Sex-Goddess with a Sex-God, and the female Virgin with the male Christ, we notice a peculiar sexual bias in his model. This is towards the projections of the male. While acknowledging that Adams took himself to be a reporter of the past, suitable adjustments in the model to incorporate the projections of the female are necessarily in order for a balanced view.

At the Great Exposition in Paris in 1900, Adams made the astonishing intellectual leap which enabled him to complete the triangulation demanded by his theory. He was in the great hall of dynamos with his friend Langley, a distinguished scientist. For Langley, a dynamo 'was but an ingenious channel.'[35] To Adams, however, it was much more than this. His Dynamo (with a capital D) was not only a symbol of the precision, power and achievement of science, it was also 'a symbol of infinity.'[36] Madame Curie had recently discovered X-rays, for example. For Adams 'the rays... were a revelation of mysterious energy like that of the Cross; they were what, in terms of medieval science, were called immediate modes of the divine substance.'[37] Or again: 'He could see only an absolute *fiat* in electricity as in faith.'[38] Here is his own account of how he began to come to terms with the Dynamo.

'As he grew accustomed to the great gallery of machines, he began to feel the forty-foot dynamos as a moral force, much as the early Christians felt the Cross. The planet itself seemed less impressive, in its old-fashioned, deliberate, annual or daily revolution, than this huge wheel, revolving within arm's-length at some vertiginous speed, and barely murmuring... while it would not wake the baby lying close against its frame.'[39] Before he left the Exposition for the last time (and he returned to it every day), he had begun to pray to the Dynamo: 'One began to pray to it.'[40] He regarded his behaviour as 'the natural expression of man before silent and infinite force.'[41] In a touching moment, he admitted 'he hugged the dynamo.'[42]

The dynamo produces electricity in reality in a way analogous to that in which the Virgin produces faith and the Venus produces desire in reality. The metallic dynamo, therefore, symbolised the entirety of the new scientific universe, especially the mathematical physics which underpinned the cosmological view of the universe so precisely. The Animated Dynamo is to be thought of as the Adams formula by which the erotic Venus, the spiritual Virgin, and the metallic Dynamo participate in each other. 'His mind was ready to feel the force of [them] all.'[43] The Animated Dynamo is therefore the model by means of which the mathematical minutiae of life participate in the sexual and spiritual minutiae of life; and *vice versa.* None own, outdo, or enclose the others. The Venus and the Virgin triangulate the Dynamo to give us the cosmos. The Dynamo in the cosmos, for its part, gives them the trigonometry to do so.

V

On the Resurrection of the Living and the Dead

'The very concept of death and resurrection lies at the heart of Christianity, while for Jews the idea of a Messiah being put to an ignominious death, and of being then raised from the dead, are quite unacceptable.' (Hugh Montefiore, *On Being A Jewish Christian*.)[1]

The idea of resurrection is notoriously difficult for many people to understand, especially those who are not Christian. Simone Weil put the matter succinctly: 'If the Gospels omitted all mention of Christ's resurrection, faith would be easier for me. The Cross by itself suffices me.'[2] She remained unbaptised. It might even be true to say that for many Christians, resurrection is an idea which has to be accepted as an article of faith, without any reaching after secular meaning. This is a pity, because it suggests the meaning of resurrection has been lost to the common ground of understanding. It is, it seems, an idea which has become so covered over by the passage of time that it has become meaningless. But this does not mean it has become dead to intellectual curiosity.

There are a number of other, related ideas which have suffered the same fate and for much the same reason. Eternal life and immortality are amongst the most conspicuous. This is not because we regard the fixed duration of a lifetime and the inevitability of death as more dominant ideas; but that, in the course of our long and bloody history, we feel we have outmoded their counterparts. We feel they are illusions of a more credulous age.

Modern psychology has taught us a great deal. One of its more significant lessons is the notion of the wish-fulfilment. We believe a thing to be true, even though we know it is not true, because we wish to believe it is true. In such a light, we are capable of asking, for example, why anybody would want to live forever; or, more cogently, what it would mean to do so. Since the idea of resurrection is indissolubly connected to the ideas of eternal life and immortality, it will be the aim of this chapter to explore resurrection as one of the key ideas in Christianity.

Montefiore tells us that, for the Jews, 'the idea of a Messiah being put to an ignominious death' is 'quite unacceptable.' The idea may have become unacceptable, but it was not always so. Take *Isaiah* chapter 53. This is 'Deutero-Isaiah' around the time of the 6th century BC, in the famous sequence of poetry called 'The Suffering Servant.'

> He was despised and rejected by others;
>   a man of suffering and acquainted with infirmity;
> and as one from whom others hide their faces
>   he was despised, and we held him of no account...
>
> He was oppressed, and he was afflicted,
>   yet he did not open his mouth;
> like a lamb that is led to the slaughter...
>
> For he was cut off from the land of the living,
>   stricken for the transgression of my people...
>
> Yet it was the will of the Lord to crush him with pain.[3]

How might the young Jesus have felt when he read that? Resolute, we might imagine. The idea of the Messiah to which Montefiore refers is much more Davidic, much more conquering King, than this. 'He [the Jewish Messiah] ushers in the time of complete blessedness. He subdues the enemies of the Jews, brings all people in subjection to Israel, and rules over all the kings and princes of the world.'[4] But the idea of a death willed, consciously and deliberately, to help rather than to hinder the righteous, is very Jewish, as *Isaiah* 53 proves beyond a doubt.

> The righteous one, my servant, shall make many righteous,
> and he shall bear their iniquities.[5]

It is also true to say that the idea of resurrection, as it was in the time of the boyhood of Jesus, is very Jewish. 'The Martyrdom of Seven Brothers' in 2 *Maccabees* 7 spells it out in exhaustive detail. Since 2 *Maccabees* is thought to have been written by a Jew in Greek around 63 BC, and to be the epitome of a larger work by Jason of Cyrene, who is otherwise unknown, any such idea, as a presence in the air, is bound to have had significance for Jesus in his formative years.[6]

The idea of resurrection for Israel as a whole first emerges in, for example, *Isaiah* 26:19:

> Your dead shall live, their corpses shall rise.
> O dwellers in the dust, awake and sing for joy!
> For your dew is a radiant dew,
> and the earth will give birth to those long dead.[7]

Or again, the loyalists of Yahweh, who have suffered for their faith, the prototypic Zionists, will rise again in the mercy of God's judgement:

> Many of those who sleep in the dust of the earth
> shall awake, some to everlasting life, and some to
> shame and everlasting contempt.[8]

Apostates, for example, are to be held in contempt. Whereas 'those who are wise shall shine like the brightness of the sky, and those who lead many to righteousness, like the stars forever and ever.'[9] The book of Daniel, which these two quotes are from, reached its final form in the time of the Greek Seleucid King Antiochus Epiphanes IV, who ruled 175-164 BC.[10]

'The Martyrdom of Seven Brothers' occurs in the presence of this king and is set in motion by him. It is necessary to understand the full context of the martyrdom to grasp the seriousness with which the Jews believed in resurrection. This is only possible by quotation.

> It happened that seven brothers and their mother were arrested and were being compelled by the king, under torture with whips and tongs, to partake of unlawful swine's flesh.[11]

Because the brothers would rather die than break a holy vow of their Jewish faith, Antiochus 'gave orders to have pans and cauldrons heated.'[12] The brother who had spoken then had his tongue cut out; he was scalped; his hands and feet were cut off; while his mother and brothers were forced to watch. 'When he was utterly helpless, the king ordered [his men] to take him to the fire, still breathing, and to fry him in a pan'.[13] All the brothers are to die such horrifying deaths. But the horror of the deaths is not the point in this context. The horror serves simply to remind us of the reality against which the Jews conceived of resurrection.

Before the second brother is tortured to death, he says to Antiochus: 'You accursed wretch, you dismiss us from this present life, but the King of the universe will raise us up to an everlasting renewal of life, because we have died for his laws.'[14] The third brother taunts Antiochus by observing, as he offers his tongue and his hands to be cut off, 'I got these from Heaven, and because of his laws I disdain them, and from him I hope to get them back again.'[15] Similar ideas are expressed by the fourth brother. The fifth says, 'Do not think that God has forsaken our people. Keep on, and see how his mighty power will torture you and your descendents.'[16] The sixth proclaims a typical Jewish idea, which runs through the prophets like a thread: 'Do not deceive yourself in vain. For we are suffering these things on our own account, because of our sins against our own God.'[17]

The mother saw all her sons tortured to death. This is what she says to honour their memory. 'I do not know how you came into being in my womb. It was not I who gave you life and breath, nor I who set in order the elements within each of you. Therefore the Creator of the world, who shaped the beginning of humankind and devised the origin of all things, will in his mercy give life and breath back to you again, since you now forget yourselves for the sake of his laws.'[18]

Here, in about as much concrete detail as we could hope for, is what the Jewish faith meant by resurrection shortly before the birth of Jesus. The fact that the sons die over the issue of eating pork is not part of our consideration.[19] This is because in his attempts to Hellenize the Jews, Antiochus stopped at nothing. If it hadn't been pork, it would have been something else. It is clear from these passages that the righteous, living strictly in accordance with the laws of God, lived in expectation of resurrection, no matter what price was exacted for their lives. The unrighteous, by contrast, living in defiance of the laws of God, could expect 'shame and everlasting contempt.'[20] *Isaiah* had long since indicated that such a hellish fate meant being eaten alive by worms that cannot die and burnt by fires that cannot go out.[21]

By the time of Christ, the idea of resurrection had reached some sort of peak. In the gospels, for example, Jesus believes in resurrection. So do the Pharisees; but the Sadducees do not. Christ's refutation of the Sadducees is clearer in *Luke* than in the other gospels, so it is there we ought to look for his idea of resurrection. He says of those resurrected from the dead: 'they cannot die anymore, because they are like angels and are children of God... And the fact that the dead are raised Moses himself showed, in the story about the bush, where he speaks of the Lord as the God of Abraham, the God of Isaac, and the God of Jacob. Now he is not God of the dead, but of the living; *for to him all of them are alive*'[22] (my italics). In other words, Moses, in talking to God in the burning bush, realises that God is talking about Abraham, Isaac, and Jacob, not as dead people, but as living beings as alive as himself. The scribes were impressed. The Sadducees were silenced.[23]

Saint Paul put the idea of resurrection squarely in the centre of the Christian faith in the mid 1st century AD. His idea of it derives from his time as a zealous Pharisee, but gains its potency from his conversion on the road to Damascus and the experiences of other early Christians. 1 *Corinthians* 15 spells out Paul's views on resurrection so succinctly, it is necessary to summarize them briefly to help the progress of our understanding.[24] The passage is also essential because of the consensus in modern scholarship which holds that the idea of resurrection found there is to be taken more seriously than that in the gospels.[25]

In Paul's mind, the resurrected Jesus Christ first appeared to Peter, the rock of the church, 'then to the twelve.' Then to another 'five hundred,' many of whom were still alive when Paul was writing his letter. Then he appeared to James. 'Last of all, as to one untimely born, he appeared also to me.'[26] Paul is not in a position to entertain doubts about the resurrection of Jesus Christ, in the light of his experience on the road to Damascus and the witness of all these people. He goes so far as to say, 'If Christ has not been raised, your faith is futile.'[27]

He gets technical when he says, 'as all die in Adam, so all will be made alive in Christ.'[28] But we know what he meant. It is the theological adage that with Adam sin and death came into being, but that with Christ forgiveness of sin and resurrection from death came into being. Christ is to put 'all his enemies under his feet. The last enemy to be destroyed is death.'[29]

Really? 'How are the dead raised? With what kind of body do they come?' 'Fool!' retorts Paul to his own question, 'What you sow does not come to life unless it dies.'[30] This is dangerously close to the dying and resurrecting gods of the Greek mystery religions, for example. Nor is there any truth in the idea that a seed dies when it is sown, before coming to life afterwards. The DNA in the seeds of plants and animals is in a continual sequence of life from one generation to another.

But there can be no doubt that Paul implies some sort of analogous sequence of life from one kind of life on earth to another kind of life in heaven.

'So it is with the resurrection of the dead. What is sown is perishable, what is raised is imperishable.'[31] What is he saying? Is it that when we die, the perishable part of us does in fact die, but that when we resurrect, the imperishable part of us does in fact live? It is the physical body which dies, the natural man, the *psychikos*, says one commentator; it is the spiritual body which lives, the spiritual man, the *pneumatikos*.[32]

Paul knew it was no use proposing that resurrected people live in un-reconstituted flesh and blood in the kingdom of heaven. It is not such flesh and blood which inherit the kingdom. It is the spirit within each of us, the spirit of the person, who is much more each of us, as it were, than such flesh and blood by itself. Such flesh and blood is present during sleep, in serious personality disorder, or after death, for example; but the person we know and love is removed from us. It is this personhood who is addressed by Paul's idea of resurrection.

When we resurrect, he says, we undergo a transformation. 'We will all be changed, in a moment, in the twinkling of an eye.'[33] When the transformation takes place, we are on the other side of death. We are no longer subject to death. As Christ said, we cannot die anymore; we are like angels; we are the children of God. The significance of 'angels' in this passage has a very ancient lineage. It is a point to which we will return. It is sufficient for the moment to say that once in this 'angelic' state, we are dead in the usual meaning of the word, but alive, if righteous, in an unkillable fashion. We are like those alive in the burning bush. It is then that we chant 'O death, where is your victory? O death, where is your sting?'[34] We are alive, if unrighteous, in an equally unkillable fashion, which scarcely bears thinking about: 'their worm shall not die, their fire shall not be quenched.'[35]

2

'Resurrection' is a Latin word translating the Greek word 'anastasis'. 'Anastasis' is not far in conceptual terms from 'ec-stasis'. 'Ec-stasis' has the

52

same meaning as the 'ecstasy' employed by the Romanian scholar Mircea Eliade in his ground-breaking work on shamanism, *Shamanism: Archaic Techniques of Ecstasy*.[36] We can discern, therefore, a strong connection between resurrection and the archaic techniques of ecstasy found in shamanism.

There is also a strong connection to be discerned between resurrection and 'Sheol'. Sheol is an important word of unknown derivation. It has been translated as 'pit', 'grave', 'hell', but is now more commonly left untranslated. The word reflects a belief in a shadowy life-after-death, as this is found in the early books of *The Old Testament*. Later Judaism refined the idea. Dante's hell in *The Divine Comedy* constitutes a very late, 13th to 14th century AD refinement of such refinement. To rise again after death is therefore the same as resurrection from Sheol.

Be this as it may, the initial concept of Sheol in early Jewish literature is anticipated by over 1000 years in the very clear picture of the underworld to be found in the Sumerian poem *The Epic of Gilgamesh*, which dates from the early third millennium BC.[37] Homer, by contrast, comes 2000 to 2200 years after *Gilgamesh*. The concepts of the underworld in the Massoretic text of *The Old Testament*, as in Homer, are demonstrably derivative of the Sumerian concept. This is not a point which has had a wide circulation. The exploration of it, however, puts us back in touch with the ancient meaning of resurrection from the dead.

In the poem *Gilgamesh* Enkidu, the friend of Gilgamesh, sees a birdman in a dream shortly before his death. The birdman is the usher into the house of the dead. In the dream, Enkidu's encounter with the birdman results in Enkidu's arms becoming covered in feathers; they become wings. He, too, is becoming birdlike. Enkidu recalls to Gilgamesh how, in the dream, the birdman 'turned his stare towards me, and he led me away to the palace [of the Queen of the Underworld], to the house from which none who enters ever returns, down the road from which there is no coming back.'[38]

Enkidu goes on, 'There is the house whose people sit in darkness; dust is their food and clay their meat. They are clothed like birds with wings for covering, they see no light, they sit in darkness. I entered the house of dust and I saw the kings of the earth, their crowns put away for ever; rulers and princes, all those who once wore kingly crowns and ruled the world in the days of old.'[39]

Enkidu relates to Gilgamesh how in his dream he saw high priests, acolytes, priests of incantation, priests of ecstasy, the god of cattle, the recorder of the gods who keeps the book of death, and many more. He saw the entire hierarchy of power in the house of the dead.[40] This is the Sumerian forerunner of the structure of Sheol, as this comes to influence Jewish and Christian concepts of hell.

Gilgamesh becomes inconsolable when Enkidu dies. Only the discovery of the secret of immortality, as this is enjoyed by the gods, affords Gilgamesh any prospect of comfort.[41] Gilgamesh is no ordinary hero. He is two thirds a god and one third human.[42] He is also the hero of a truly epic poem. Suitably equipped, he sets out on his quest for immortality. This is by no means only for himself, but for his friend Enkidu and ordinary humanity as well.[43] In this context, it is pointless to ascribe Paul's influence on Christianity, as some have done, as too Hellenistic, too suggestive of the dying and resurrecting gods of the mystery religions, and too little in the true Jewish tradition.[44] From the perspective of *Gilgamesh*, which came into being in its written form shortly after writing itself,[45] both the Greeks and the Israelites, not to mention the Assyrians and the Babylonians, served as conduits for the conceptual apparatus of the underworld. It makes no difference, therefore, which school of thought we follow to come to terms with the word 'resurrection'. All agree Paul's influence on Christianity has been colossal; but it cannot be separated from his affirmation of the ancient, pre-Jewish meaning of the word.

Some of the coincidences between *Gilgamesh* and the gospels 3000 years later offer us clues to the meaning of resurrection. They also prove the ancient durability of the idea. The principal clues seem to be these.

(1)   God ('the father of the gods') gives Gilgamesh 'power to bind and to loose.'[46] This idea is found in the Massoretic text, as well as in *Matthew* 16:19, for example. Jesus says to Peter near Caesarea Philippi, 'I will give you the keys of the kingdom of heaven, and whatever you bind on earth will be bound in heaven, and whatever you loose on earth will be loosed in heaven.'[47] This is the topos of power from heaven to be used on earth.

(2)   God gives Gilgamesh the power to be 'the darkness and the light of mankind.'[48] Christ says to his disciples, 'You are the light of the world.'[49] And 'I am the light of the world.'[50] This is the topos of the power from heaven operating on earth.

(3)   God gives Gilgamesh 'unexampled supremacy' over his people.[51] Jesus says to his disciples after his resurrection, 'All authority in heaven and on earth has been given to me.'[52] This topos represents the aspect of authority in all matters to do with church and government. It is an authority which comes from God, not man. It is the sacred authority which governs the human estate. This means that once established, *mutatis mutandis*, it is a natural target for the power of evil.

(4)   With the help of the gods, Gilgamesh and Enkidu work together to overcome the power of evil. They achieve this.[53] Christ says 'I have

overcome the world.'[54] This is the topos of the victory of the power of God over the power of evil.

(5)   Apart from the death of Enkidu, Gilgamesh is also brought to despair by ordinary human mortality. He sees 'the bodies floating on the river.'[55] The sting of death is as yet by no means immaterial. The pain of it strengthens his resolve in his search for immortality.[56] This bears comparison with Christ's compassion on meeting a leper,[57] for example, or weeping when he hears of the death of Lazarus.[58] This is the topos of the spiritual hero visibly affected by the misery of human life.

(6)   Gilgamesh is not led astray by Ishtar. Ishtar is an earlier form of Astarte or the Queen of Heaven. She makes a blatant attempt to seduce him, going as far as to say, 'grant me seed of your body'.[59] But because of his unhappiness about death, this most powerful sex goddess, precursor of the even more powerful Diana of the Ephesians, is powerless.[60] This represents the topos of the overcoming of temptation. We see the parallel in the temptation of Jesus in the wilderness by the devil.[61]

(7)   The gate which opens on the threshold of the dead, which Enkidu describes to Gilgamesh, is guarded by the birdman.[62] This birdman can be viewed in a direct line of descent from the birdman known to us from the world-famous cave paintings in Lascaux. Lascaux is close to the Vézère river in the Périgord region of France. The particular painting in question in the cave dates from 15,070 BC plus or minus 130 years.[63] Judging by the quality of the paintings discovered in the Chauvet cave in Vallon-Pont-d'Arc in the nearby region of Ardèche in 1995, which have been carbon-dated to 30,340 to 32,410 years before the present, it does not seem unreasonable to extend this line of descent that much further back.[64] Henry de Lumley, director of the National Museum of Natural

History in France, said of the Chauvet paintings: 'the way animals are drawn... is evidence of something sacred.'[65] Because of the close association between the birdman, the shaman, and the sacerdotal, this remark does not come as a surprise.

The topos of the birdman as shaman, and *vice versa*, is the topos of the one who knows the secrets of death. The feathers and wings of the birdman, for example, with their explicit implication of flight, have a long and venerable tradition in our past. They are seen in angels, of course, but also in cherubim, sphinxes, griffins, and the winged figure of Nike or Victory found on Greek funeral urns. The prospect of flight suggests the prospect of transcendence over death, or resurrection. Monumental sculptures of Gilgamesh with wings, holding the herb of immortality, are also common.[66] The motif of feathers, wings, and spiritual flight is in fact ubiquitous.

The poem which bears Gilgamesh's name gives us direct insight into the meaning of the birdman. The birdman is the shaman in his spiritual aspect. The birdman is an image of our guide to spiritual reality. Questions about the existence of such matters are open-ended at the best of times, but they become, as we see in the case of Enkidu, unavoidable at the approach of death.

Christ is unequivocal in his approach to death. 'I am the bread of life,' he says.[67] 'I am the resurrection and the life. Those who believe in me, even though they die, will live, and everyone who lives and believes in me will never die.'[68] If we think of Christ as the archetypal shaman in his life on earth, and as the archetypal birdman in his subsequent ministry during the last two millennia, we will have some idea of the necessity of getting to grips with his idea of resurrection. 'I am the resurrection.'

Christ is the mightiest image of the birdman possessed by the Christian religion. Without a doubt, the second mightiest image must be that in the first chapter of *Ezekiel*. The vision of the winged cherubim depicted there, supporting the throne of God, is so amazing, so conscious, so full of eyes and fire, denoting life, and so exalted, it is difficult to grasp its meaning at all. Yet in this vision the Jewish genius for spirituality surpassed itself. Outside the vision of Christ in majesty, no more awesome or terrifying an image of the birdman is to hand. What is more, it seems far from unreasonable to think that Ezekiel's vision of 'the appearance of the likeness of the glory of the Lord' had a profound influence on Jesus Christ himself.[69]

(8) The birdman in *Gilgamesh* is a figure who knows the way in and the way out of Sheol. Enkidu's description of him is worth our attention:

> The heavens roared, and earth rumbled back an answer; between them stood I before an awful being, the sombre-faced man-bird; he had directed on me his purpose. His was a vampire face, his foot was a lion's foot, his hand was an eagle's talon. He fell on me and his claws were in my hair, he held me fast and I smothered; then he transformed me so that my arms became wings covered with feathers.[70]

This is a figure seen in a dream. He has all the power and autonomy of an archetypal form. He can come and go in the house of the dead. He is, in effect, one of the gods and goddesses of the Sumerian underworld. The Queen of the Underworld has a secretary, a 'recorder of the gods' who 'keeps the book of death.'[71] These awesome beings are therefore directly linked to Dilmun, the Sumerian paradise, the home of the king of the gods.

Christ made it repeatedly clear to his disciples that he would be killed, that he would die, that he would go to hell; but that on the third day he would rise from the dead and ascend to heaven.[72] The cherubim of Ezekiel give us some idea of how this ascent might be affected. Once understood, they reveal access to a virtually infinite potency, subject only to the will of God. Resurrecting a world from Sheol would stretch their capabilities scarcely at all. So there is in the Jewish tradition which Christ inherited both the idea of resurrection and the means for carrying it out. This is the topos of the genuine possibility of resurrection, as this is conceived by Gilgamesh, Ezekiel, and Jesus Christ.

(9)   The agony of Gilgamesh over the death of his friend Enkidu, his own death, and death itself, articulates our inability to live happily in the face of death ourselves. To search for an answer to this is therefore in the human interest. This is the topos of inquiry itself. We want to know more than we do, because what we do know is not enough. This is not simply a question of satisfying the curiosity of the innocent and the naïve. It is a question of satisfying the curiosity of those who have witnessed the worst kind of atrocities, whether perpetrated by man or nature. The mature and experienced witness is therefore nothing other than the intelligent general reader.

To satisfy his own curiosity, Gilgamesh goes in search of immortality. To satisfy our curiosity, Christ offers this perpetual message: 'Come to me, all you that are weary... and I will give you rest. Take my yoke upon you, and learn from me... For my yoke is easy, and my burden is light.'[73] We are assured on the point: 'Blessed are those who mourn, for they will be comforted.'[74] Just as Christ's inquiry into death did not stop at death, or shrink before it, so we are invited to follow him through death to the kingdom of heaven beyond it.

There is no essential difference between the Sumerian paradise and the Christian heaven, if we limit our considerations to the idea that both are the location of immortality. But whereas Gilgamesh fails in his bid to get there, the resurrection of Christ is clearly meant as an indication of his success. We will return to this point.

(10)   In the world in which Gilgamesh lives, the universal pool of myth, legend, and tradition is immediately brought into play to improve his chances of success. He seeks out Utnapishtim, 'the Faraway', because he has heard the legend about him. This is that Utnapishtim has entered 'the assembly of the gods' and is the only human being to have done so. In Gilgamesh's eyes, Utnapishtim is therefore the only mortal to have achieved immortality.[75] Like Noah a millennium after him, he was also the sole survivor of The Flood.[76] He lives in 'the garden of the sun', 'the land of Dilmun', the Sumerian paradise – a clear precursor of Eden and the Christian paradise.[77]

This topos ties in with the use made of oral and written tradition by Christ in the world in which he lives. 'You have heard it said...' 'It is written...' For example, 'It is written, One does not live by bread alone but by every word that comes from the mouth of God.' Which is *Matthew* 4:4 quoting directly from *Deuteronomy* 8:3.[78] In this topos, tradition points the way to the meaning of resurrection.

(11)   The route to the assembly of the gods in the land of Dilmun is hard, exacting, dangerous, and uncertain.[79] This is the topos of the dark night of the soul. We see it in the agony in the garden of Gethsemane.[80] We see it in its most spectacular form in the crucifixion.[81] The expectation that understanding the word 'resurrection' is easy, either to believe in it or to dismiss it, is consequently naïve.

(12)   'The holy things, the things of stone' must not be broken. Unfortunately for Gilgamesh, he smashes them.[82] Since they have something to do with the birdman, which is not explained, this is a bad move, which is also unexplained.[83] This is the topos of deviating from the straight and narrow, because of which achievement of the aim of the sacred purpose is lost. The idea of the holy stones and their link with immortality through the birdman is a tantalizing forerunner of the stone tablets on which the Ten Commandments and the laws of God are written, as we have these in the Five Books of Moses or the Pentateuch. Resurrection from the dead through belief in, and righteous observance of, the Torah, which is the Pentateuch 'and the whole body of Judaism's religious-ethical literature', is axiomatic in the Jewish religion.[84] [85]

This topos says, Do not break the laws of God; you do so at your peril. Christ's adhesion to these laws is best seen, prior to the crucifixion, in the agony in the garden. 'Father, if you are willing, remove this cup from me; yet, not my will but yours be done.'[86] This, the topos of obedience, is also the topos of vigilance. The failure of his most intimate disciples to be vigilant on such a night draws this remark: 'Why are you sleeping? Get up and pray that you may not come into the time of trial.'[87] This is the topos which is to be Gilgamesh's undoing, when it returns at a later stage.

(13)   One of the most important matters associated with 'the holy things, the things of stone' is not lost on Gilgamesh. This is that unbridled evil in the world will result in its extinction. Gilgamesh learns of this from Utnapishtim, who tells him that the gods ordained extinction once before, and for the same reason, when they sent The Flood.[88] Utnapishtim then tells him the story of The Flood. Because 'the world bellowed like a wild bull,' and because 'the uproar of mankind is intolerable,' the gods could get no sleep. 'So the gods agreed to exterminate mankind.'[89]

Foreknowledge of such a catastrophe is essential to escape extinction. It becomes the *sine qua non* of salvation. This is the topos of redemption. Gilgamesh will win the quest for immortality if he follows Utnapishtim's instructions. Christ says, 'I came not to judge the world, but to save the world.'[90] 'Salvation is from the Jews.'[91] When the woman of Samaria says to him, 'I know that Messiah is coming,' he says, 'I am he.'[92] Faced with extinction of one kind or another, redemption from it becomes vital.

(14)   The forces that shape the lives of Gilgamesh and his people, the gods, can be propitiated by sweet-smelling sacrifices. Utnapishtim made such a sacrifice immediately after he had survived The Flood.[93] To read this account of The Flood and its aftermath is to realise that in the account of Noah and The Flood in *Genesis* chapters 6-8, which dates from 1000 years later, the very text seems to borrow from *Gilgamesh*. Noah's sacrifice after The Flood, for example, follows Utnapishtim's, as in 'the Lord smelled the pleasing odour' in *Genesis* and 'the gods smelled the sweet savour' in *Gilgamesh*.[94] Gilgamesh, like Noah, does everything he can to get divine power on his side. This is the topos of propitiation.

The willing self-sacrifice of Jesus Christ is uniquely sweet-smelling to God in the Christian tradition, because the sacrificer and the sacrificed are the same. Christians believe that in the crucifixion the topos of propitiation consummates itself.[95] The Last Supper spells out the meaning of this:

> While they were eating, Jesus took a loaf of bread, and after blessing it he broke it, gave it to the disciples, and said 'Take, eat; this is my body.' Then he took a cup, and after giving thanks he gave it to them, saying, 'Drink from it, all of you; for this is my blood of the covenant, which is poured out for many for the forgiveness of sins.'[96]

There is no account of the Last Supper in *John*, but 'The Bread from Heaven' passage in it touches on the same theme. While teaching in the synagogue in Capernaum, Jesus says:

> Very truly, I tell you, unless you eat the flesh of the Son of Man and drink his blood, you have no life in you. Those who eat my flesh and drink my blood have eternal life... Just as the living Father sent me, and I live because of the Father, so whoever eats me will live because of me. This is the bread that came down from heaven... the one who eats this bread will live forever.[97]

There can be no getting away from the meaning of such passages. It is spelt out in one sentence: 'For God so loved the world that he gave his only Son, so that everyone who believes in him may not perish but may have eternal life.'[98]

This topos suggests the efficacious interaction between the divine reality of God and the human reality of man. The interaction is made efficacious, it ought to be said, though the offices of the sacrificer, the one who *makes sacred*, who sacrifices himself, who therefore *makes himself sacred.* By believing in him, we believe in the sacred opening he has made in this way for us to reach the divine reality of God. Disbelief in him is therefore essentially disbelief in the one who makes sacred, who makes himself sacred for our benefit. In this context, to decline any serious meaning to the word 'resurrection' is to decline any serious meaning to the one who makes sacred, who makes himself sacred for our benefit. It is, therefore, to decline any serious meaning to the divine reality of God.

It is worth noticing that the archaic techniques of the shaman devolve onto the idea of 'making sacred'. When we confront his spiritual aspect in the birdman, we have, as it were, already passed through such 'sacrificial' actions. To be a Christian, therefore, is to believe in Jesus Christ as the 'sacrificer' who 'sacrifices himself' to 'make us sacred' for our benefit. So he is the quintessential birdman whose flight through the world of the spirit is wholly in the human interest. A Christian is one who is 'on board.'

(15) Utnapishtim tells Gilgamesh that if he wants the help of the gods to achieve immortality, this is to demand absolute vigilance of himself. Gilgamesh agrees to this final test.[99] He has, after all, reached Dilmun or paradise through the exercise of his godlike powers and human heroism. He is still mortal, however, as indicated by the animal skins he is wearing.[100] Utnapishtim agrees to call a full assembly of the gods, who, acting as one, have the power to do anything whatsoever.[101]

Immortality is not a problem. Nor is the resurrection of the living and the dead. The problem is this: 'Only prevail against sleep for six days and seven nights.' Vigilance, in other words. 'A mist of sleep like soft wool teased from the fleece' overtakes Gilgamesh. He has failed. When he wakes up, he knows he has failed. 'What shall I do, O Utnapishtim? Already the thief in the night [death] has hold of my limbs, death inhabits my room.' [102] We have seen the topos of obedience and vigilance; this is the topos of vigilance and failure. Christ comes close to it in the agony in the garden of Gethsemane: 'In his anguish he prayed more earnestly, and his sweat became like great drops of blood falling down on the ground.'[103] The thought of his forthcoming death gets to him in no uncertain terms. How can he possibly have the courage to go through with it?

Christ also comes close to failure on the cross. 'About three o'clock Jesus cried with a loud voice... "My God, my God, why have you forsaken me?"'[104] But since this is a direct quotation from the first verse of *Psalm* 22 and a conscious echo of the first verse of *Psalm* 10, it seems more reasonable to suppose that being absolutely forsaken by God, seeing God's absolute hiddenness in the time of trouble, is nothing less than the most harrowing part of his making sacred.[105] In any case, Christians believe Christ did not fail. Their religion rests on the point.

(16)   After his failure to pass the final test, Gilgamesh is unable to draw on the infinite power of the assembly of the gods. He is obliged to quit paradise, having failed in his quest for immortality.[106] If Christ is a tragic success, Gilgamesh is a heroic failure. As he is leaving Dilmun, Utnapishtim's wife, who lives in the orbit of her husband's immortality, takes pity on him. He is offered a consolation prize. This is a prickly underwater plant, something like a rose, which restores youth to the old. It does not bestow immortality, but a shadow of it.[107]

Gilgamesh is delighted by the idea of returning to his home city, Uruk in the Mesopotamian basin, to give the plant to the city elders. This helps to offset his sense of failure. But while he is bathing, a snake snatches the plant from him. 'I found a sign and now I have lost it,' he sighs. Lack of vigilance has let him down again.[108] He no longer possesses even the psychoactive plant as a sign of how close he came to success. The snake is an evident precursor of the serpent in the Garden of Eden, who robs Adam and Eve of the fruit of the tree of life.[109] This is the topos of the fall from grace. The topoi of the two ancient traditions are beginning to converge.

(17)   The failure to obtain immortality means that Gilgamesh must return to Uruk to die. He begins to realise this may not be an ignominious end. In fact, his failure is seen by his people as heroic on an epic scale.[110] This is one reason why the poem remains so readable after 5000 years, in N. K. Sandar's imaginative and selective reconstruction in her own richly

inventive and strongly narrative prose, made up from the ancient poetic sources, which have come down to us on assorted and by no means undamaged cuneiform tablets. But the equating of failure with death is a sharp reminder of that other equation: 'The wages of sin is death.'[111] This is the topos of death as failure to come to terms with the meaning of resurrection.

(18)   Bread offerings and wine libations form an essential element in the ceremony surrounding the death of Gilgamesh. The priests make bread offerings for the Keeper of the Gate, the birdman, whom we recall from Enkidu's dream.[112] Bread offerings are also made to 'the god of the serpent', who is identical with 'the lord of the Tree of Life.'[113] Bread offerings and wine libations are made to the ancestral gods, and all the other gods, the entire 'host of heaven.'[114]

This is a millennium in advance of the bread and wine offerings made by the priest and king Melchizedek, the prototype of the priest in the Judeo-Christian tradition.[115] This is the topos of thanksgiving. The word 'eucharist', for example, comes from the Greek word 'efkaristo', the present everyday word for 'thank you'. The Sumerians thanked the gods for the life of Gilgamesh. But they did not want his soul to sit in the house of the dead, eating dust and clay, clothed like a bird in the darkness. They wanted the gods to give air to his wings and transport him to paradise, but they knew their wish was in vain, for the father of the gods had said: 'You [Gilgamesh] were given the kingship, such was your destiny, everlasting life was not your destiny.'[116] Lamentation and thanksgiving are combined. When Melchizedek blest Abram, who became Abraham, the great patriarchal figure of Judaism, Christianity, and Islam, he did so to thank Abram for helping in the rout of his enemies.[117] The topos of thanksgiving ties in with the topos of propitiation to strengthen the bond between god and man.

(19)   In the Sumerian ritual, the identification of bread and wine with thanksgiving and propitiation is obvious.[118]   When Christ identifies the bread and the wine in the Last Supper with his body and his blood, he is not simply reiterating the Hellenistic mystery religions, as some scholars like Hyam Maccoby have imagined.[119]   Christ is making it clear, amongst other things, that he is entering on his own quest for immortality. He is attempting to succeed where Gilgamesh has failed. This is not to suggest Christ knew the poem; but it had been in the air he breathed for 3000 years, both widely disseminated and hugely popular.[120]   If *The Iliad* and *The Odyssey* influence us today, they are roughly as distant from us as Christ was from *Gilgamesh*.

The crucial difference between the failure of Gilgamesh and the success of Christ can be summed up in their different relationships with sacrifice. The bread and wine sacrifice is offered *for* Gilgamesh after his death. The bread and wine sacrifice is offered *by* Christ before his death. In the case of Gilgamesh, the sacrifice thanks the gods and speeds his soul with their help to paradise. In the case of Christ, the sacrifice is a symbol of the self-sacrifice to come: I will die, but I will do so to break the circle of life and death, to break the circle of crime and punishment. My death becomes a symbol of forgiveness, a symbol of the way out of Sheol. When you say 'Do this in remembrance of me' during the Eucharist, I ask you to remember the immortality I achieved for myself for your benefit.[121]

To become the door to immortal life, indicated by the words, 'I am the way, and the truth, and the life,'[122] 'I am the resurrection and the life,'[123] Christ proceeded to Golgotha, 'The Place of the Skull.'[124]   Absolute vigilance was called for, as we have seen. Did he succeed where Gilgamesh failed? Did he in fact achieve resurrection and the immortality or eternal life he promised to those who believed in him? We recall Paul's remark to the Corinthians: 'If Christ has not been raised, your faith is futile.' So a Christian trusts Paul, trusts the apostles, trusts the saints and numerous others, on the pivotal point that the ancient quest for immortality was indeed accomplished by Jesus of Nazareth. His vigilance was up to it. This is the topos of faith in the spiritual hero.

(20)   Just as the bread and wine offered by the Sumerian priests for Gilgamesh propitiate 'the gods of the serpent, the lord of the Tree of Life,' so the bread and wine offered by Christ, his body and blood, propitiate God, in his role as the supreme authority over the serpent in the Garden of Eden. The body and blood of Christ propitiate God in his role as the supreme authority over Satan, the Evil One, which is to say the actual nature of evil and the actual nature of death. The meaning of Christ's propitiation of God is therefore indistinguishable from the meaning of resurrection. Both point to the release from evil and death in the world.

When Christ proclaims he is the door to the living God, this bears an equivalence in meaning to a shaman offering the archaic techniques of ecstasy to transport us to the world of the birdman. This is because the birdman is the usher to the house of the dead, through which we proceed to the land of the living gods. This is the topos of the value of resurrection.

The topos implies, therefore, that resurrection is as relevant to the living as the dead. This is a view shared by *The Tibetan Book of the Dead*, for example, which was first committed to writing in the time of Padma Sambhava in the 8th century AD. The point is emphasized by Lama

Anagarika Govinda in his foreword.[125] W. Y. Evans-Wentz, the renowned editor of the book, made the additional point that *The Egyptian Book of the Dead* is also to be read in this way. Both books express 'the Art of Dying and Coming Forth into a New Life.' What both Lama Govinda and Evans-Wentz meant by this idea is plain: the art of dying is to be practised as much while living as while dying. For Evans-Wentz, in fact, to practise the art of dying successfully was to experience 'the ever-recurrent Resurrection.'[126] The value of resurrection, therefore, touches the very heart of the art of living.

(21) Having propitiated God so that God does indeed exercise his authority over evil and death, it remains only for Christ, the archetypal shaman and the archetypal birdman, to guide us through Sheol towards the fruit of the Tree of Life. This is now rid of 'the god of the serpent,' because of Christ's propitiation of God with his own body and blood. The topoi of the two ancient traditions converge at this point.

(22) This leaves the most important topos of all. What in *Gilgamesh* is called immortality and in the gospels eternal life is achieved by what we call resurrection. This amounts to sharing in the existence of God, including his authority over evil and death. This means that to contemplate the meaning of resurrection is nothing other than to contemplate the meaning of the living God.

VI

The Foundation Sacrifice of the Dorian Greek Nation

Mycenean culture, derivative of Minoan Crete, took root in Greece about 2100 BC. Mycenean palaces later flourished in places such as Mycenae, Tiryns, Thebes, and Pylos, between 1600 and 1200 BC. The dates of the Trojan War are uncertain, but the Greeks traditionally date the destruction of Troy to 1184 BC. Mycenae was finally wiped out by 1150 BC. There is reason to believe the Dorian Greeks arrived in Greece in earnest around 1200-1100 BC.[1] Pelops, Atreus, Agamemnon, Clytemnestra, and Orestes, for example, were Myceneans. It is possible, but not certain, that unlike the Dorian Greeks they were not Indo-European.[2] Homer and Hesiod, by contrast, who date from roughly 750-700 BC, were Indo-European Dorian Greeks. By their time, the first Olympic Games had been held in 776 BC, and the Greek alphabet was in formation from its Phoenician original.[3] The indications are that the Dorian Greeks took over Mycenean Greece, destroying Mycenean culture in the process.[4] The Greece of Olympia and Delphi, Homer and Hesiod, Heraclitus and Parmenides, Aeschylus and Sophocles, Pericles and Alcibiades, Herodotus and Thuycidides, was Dorian. The Parthenon itself, pride of the Dorian Greek nation, was not begun until 447 BC, nineteen years before the birth of Plato in 428 BC.[5] So how did the Dorian Greek nation as we know it, and which has given us so much, come into being?

We know it is of Indo-European stock and invaded Greece from the north.[6] We know it had no words for 'sea', 'island', 'bath', 'hyacinth', 'mint', 'terebinth', 'narcissus', and 'acanthus', for example; and practically no words for metals or metal-working.[7] We also know 'in Greek most names for musical instruments, and even those of many poetical forms, such as elegy, hymn, iambus, are loanwords from languages which were not Indo-European.'[8] We know, therefore, the Dorian Greek nation had a genius for assimilating, adapting, and advancing on, what it met. It not only did this with the Phoenician alphabet, but also with Mycenean metal-work in gold and bronze, Egyptian sculpture, and Babylonian mathematics, for example.[9]

If we look into the early history of the Greeks, we come across the word 'Pelasgian'. This meant a great deal to the Cambridge scholar John Cuthbert Lawson in 1909, but by 1971 it had become more or less meaningless to the poet, scholar, and archaeologist Peter Levi.[10] Why? If we turn to the index in Pausanias's great work *Guide to Greece*, translated and edited by Peter Levi, we find eight entries under the word.[11] Pausanias, who was active in the mid 2nd century AD, was a doctor, traveller, and geographer. It has been said of him: 'His accuracy is confirmed by existing remains.'[12] What he has to tell us about the word 'Pelasgian', in the light of Peter Levi's brilliant commentary, is eye-opening.

When discussing Arcadia, Pausanias said: 'The Arcadians say the first inhabitant of this country was Pelasgos.'[13] He quoted the post-Homeric, late 7th to early 6th century BC poet Asios of Samos.

And black earth produced god-equalling Pelasgos in mountains with long hair of tall trees that a mortal race might come to be.[14]

Pausanias added: 'They say in the reign of Pelasgos the country came to be called Pelasgia.'[15] Pelasgia, in its turn, came to be called Arcadia, by these means: 'in the second generation after Pelasgos the country increased its number of cities and its human population,' Pausanias said.[16] Niktimos succeeded Pelasgos's son Lykaon. Arkas succeeded him. 'It was his [Arkas's] reign that gave the people their name of Arcadians instead of Pelasgians.'[17]

These Pelasgians or Arcadians of Pausanias are not to be confused with the native, aboriginal inhabitants of Peloponnese, who are also called Pelasgians.[18] So a point of clarification must be made here. 'A complex

"Pelasgian question" was started by classical Greeks, through the practise of using "Pelasgian" in any part of the Aegean world, as a synonym of aborigines.'[19] The Arcadians to whom Pausanias is referring are demonstrably not aborigines, but the Dorian Greeks. This will become obvious when we notice their chief god, their characteristic games, and their archaeological remains.

Pelasgos, as we have seen, had a son called Lykaon. Pausanias went on: 'Pelasgos's son Lykaon... founded the city of Lykosaura on Mount Lykaon and named Lykaon Zeus and instituted the Lykaon games.'[20] When Pausanias was actually in Lycosaura, he noted: 'A little higher up is the circuit wall of Lycosaura, which has a few inhabitants. Lycosaura is the oldest of all the cities the earth and its islands have produced: it was the first city the sun ever saw. It was from here that the rest of mankind learnt to build cities.'[21] This is, of course, absolute nonsense. But it is revealing that Pausanias should express himself in this way. He clearly knew nothing about the much more ancient city of Jericho and its massive stone walls dating from around 8000 BC;[22] or of 'Uruk, the strong walled city,' which the historical Gilgamesh ruled around 2700-2500 BC.[23] But he did know about 'the walls of Babylon' and 'Memnon's walls at Sousa in Persia,' for example. Peter Levi tells us 'Pausanias gets his idea of the walls of Babylon from Herodotus's amazing description.'[24] Herodotus saw Babylon for himself and said it 'surpasses in splendour any city of the known world' in his time.[25] He was active in the third quarter of the 5th century BC. So whatever else he was doing, Pausanias was projecting the foundation of Lycosaura well back before this.

For him, the people who built Lycosaura, instituted the Lykaon games, and named Zeus as their supreme god, were the sons and daughters of Pelasgos, Lykaon, Nyktimos, and Arkas.[26] The archaeology of Arcadia as he knew it around 150 AD, walking among the numerous ruins, was the product of his own Dorian Greeks. He thought of them as the builders of Lycosaura, 'the oldest of all the cities the earth and its islands have produced... the first city the sun ever saw.'[27] The very fuzziness of his sense of the historical past allows us to place him in our own with some ease.

In order to clarify the reasons for his sense of his Dorian Greek origins, there was nothing to do but to go out and explore Lycosaura and Mount Lykaon *in situ*. These places were self-evidently the keys to his conception of the founding of his own nation. What did they have to reveal to us? On Sunday 31st January 1999, I drove to the market place in Kopanaki in Messinias, which abuts on Arcadia, to meet a Greek acquaintance, Sophia Bertram. After inspecting maps, the *Guide to Greece*, and *The Sacred Executioner* by Hyam Maccoby, an expert on foundation sacrifice,[28] we drove towards Megalopolis, then west towards Lycosaura and Mount Lykaon. By 1.30pm, we were in the site of ancient Lycosaura. Standing there, on an officially sacred mound under an oak-tree, the visual majesty of the place, inspired by the mountains and valleys around it, warranted emotions of the profoundest kind. A sense of reverence seemed the most natural thing in the world. This had nothing to do with the Mycenean, Achaian, or Dorian Greek religions. It had to do with the location of the site itself. I crossed myself.

The phrase 'under every green tree' came to mind from the Massoretic text. This phrase was used there, especially by the prophets, as in *Isaiah*, *Jeremiah*, and *Ezekiel*, to signal alien religious practices in just such a place under just such a tree.[29] But the antiquity of the site, as a purely geographical phenomenon, stretched back to a time before *The Old Testament* text was written; to a time long before the Mycenean, Achaian, or Dorian Greeks had come into being. That was the beauty of the place. There was a sense of holy ground. It was not for nothing that the oldest Dorian city of Pausanias's imagination had been said by him to have been founded on it. There was no substitute for being there to see this. And all around were the massive cut stones indicating the unmistakable presence of the Dorian Greeks. In comparison with the geography of the place, they looked like recent arrivals.

The site was a natural temple. There seemed no need to cut stones or build buildings. It was the kind of place Abraham might have tried to sacrifice Isaac.[30] It was the kind of place where 'sacrifice' or 'making sacred' seemed like a logical extension of itself.

So Lycosaura was impressive enough. What did Pausanias, Levi, and Maccoby between them have to tell us about Mount Lykaon above it? 'To the left of the sanctuary [of Lycosaura] is Mount Lykaon *which some of the Arcadians call Olympos, and the Holy Peak. They say Zeus was raised on this mountain*'[31] (my italics). Zeus was doubtless raised on many a mountain, but was there a possibility that Mount Lykaon predated Mount Olympos as the foundation site of the Dorian gods? Did the Lykaon games predate the Olympic games? This seemed unlikely, because Pausanias told us, 'They [the Dorian Athenians] trace back the Olympic games to before the beginning of the human race.'[32] But he also told us that in his view the Lykaon games predated the Athenian games.[33] Whatever the case, the Lykaon games were 'early' by Dorian standards, and Mount Lykaon had some crucial significance in the founding of Dorian Greek society. As we approached it, it was easy to see why: an awesome white mountain towered above us.

We drove up a narrow, twisting road through several villages. What lay ahead, beyond the last village, was frightening. This was because of the time of year. It was not a good idea to drive up such a mountain in the middle of winter. The road climbed steeply. The panorama over the valley of the Alpheos and the plain of Megalopolis induced vertigo. As we ascended, now well above the snowline, the track grew narrower, steeper, whiter. There was no barrier at the edge. There was no turning back or reversing. In the circumstances, that would have been even more dangerous. It seemed quite possible that the car would slide sideways and backwards off the road at any moment. There was a drop of several thousand feet. Suddenly the snow white summit of Mount Lykaon came into view.

74

The road levelled as it entered a small, flat plain. The danger was over, but only for a time. The descent would be as dangerous as the ascent. It was 3pm and we were near the top, which stood 1421 metres above sea level. We saw a sign sticking from the snow which said we were in the ancient stadium. What was a stadium doing there? 'In ancient times,' Pausanius informed us, 'they held the Lykaon festival here... There is a sanctuary of Pan on Lykaon with a grove of trees around it and a stadium for horse-racing in front of it. There are pedestals for portrait statues there, though the figures have gone.'[34] We saw cut stone slabs and pillars beneath the snow. The stadium itself was a lake of snow, pure white, not a flake moving.

The tremendous mountainhead, draped in a mantle of snow, peered down on us. Looking up at the Holy Peak in the sunlight, it was not difficult to imagine our reception if we overstayed our welcome. But first we inquired into its dreadful, pristine holiness. 'There are some amazing things on Mount Lykaon,' Pausanias said, 'but the most astounding of all was this. There is a precinct of Lykaon Zeus on the mountain, which no person is allowed to enter. If you disregard this law and go in it is absolutely certain that you will die within the year.'[35] Why 'within a year' will become clear. 'On the highest peak of the mountain is a mound of earth which is an altar of Lykaon Zeus, *from which you can see most of the Peloponnese*'[36] (my italics). So what we had here, in retrospective vision, was the leaders of the Dorian Greek nation on this very summit, sometime around 1200 BC, surveying the Peloponnese, the new found land of their people, after the long trek from the north. It was, of course, axiomatic that a sacrifice had to be made to the chief of the gods to thank him for delivering the nation. And what a glorious, rich land they could see around them. Too bad about the resident Myceneans.

The annual sacrifice was performed somewhat lower down, on the altar in the sanctuary of Zeus the Deliverer, to whom mountain summits were sacred.[37] Pausanias: 'At this altar they offered a *secret sacrifice* to Lykaon Zeus. *I could see no pleasure in pursuing inquiries about this sacrifice*'[38] (my italics). Peter Levi commented: 'The race-track was found by Kourouniotis [in 1903]. It is in a small valley a little below the peak, called Kato Kampos. An inscribed list of winners at the Lykaon games in the late 4th century BC was found in 1905. The games were very elaborate, and the winners include an Athenian, Argives, Spartans, and Arkarnanians.'[39]

We came to the crunch. Peter Levi enlightened us: 'Kourouniotis examined the altar [in the sanctuary of Zeus], which contained a lot of bones, two iron knives, and some bronze tripods; and later excavated the sanctuary which yielded some fine small bronzes, including a splendid two-headed bronze snake... *The secret sacrifice was human*'[40] (my italics).

We were in a classic foundation sacrifice site, such as discussed at length by Hyam Maccoby.[41] The point about this particular site was the strong possibility of it being the foundation sacrifice site of the Dorian Greek nation itself, when it chose to settle in the Peloponnese. That was why Pausanias had picked up the local wisdom about Lycosaura on Mount Lykaon being 'the first city the sun ever saw. It was from here that the rest of mankind [read 'the Dorian Greek nation'] learnt to build cities.'[42] That was why Lycosaura was 'the oldest of all the cities the earth and its islands have produced.'[43] Was it on this Holy Peak that the Dorian Greek nation with its famous philosophers, poets, historians, and politicians staked its original claim to the sovereignty of the land? If there were rival places in the Peloponnese with such claims, none could command such a site high up in the centre of the peninsula with such an extraordinary historical aura around it.

There was a further dimension to the site, which aroused imagination. Pausanias told us that Pelasgos had a son called Lykaon. He said of Lykaon: 'He founded the city of Lycosaura on Mount Lykaon and named Lykaon Zeus and instituted the Lykaon games.'[44] What did Lykaon mean?

'Lykaon brought a human child to the altar of Lykaon Zeus, slaughtered it and poured its blood on the altar.'[45] As we shall see, Pausanias was not too happy when he learnt about this. Why was Lykaon called 'Lykaon', which means 'wolf'? What was the connection with 'lycanthropy', which means 'wolfman', and is defined as 'a kind of insanity described by ancient writers in which the patient imagines himself to be a wolf' or as 'the kind of witchcraft which was supposed to consist in the assumption by human beings of the form and nature of wolves'?[46] What does it mean that 'lycanthrope' is a synonym of 'werewolf'? The answers to these questions were about to become obvious. They clearly had something to do with the word *Lykaon*.

Pausanias told us that 'they say at that sacrifice he [Lykaon] was suddenly turned into a wolf.'[47] Pausanias also told us that he personally believed in this legend 'told in Arcadia from ancient times.'[48] These were the details of the legend. 'They say that after Lykaon someone was always turned into a wolf at the [annual] sacrifice of Lykaon Zeus, but not for his whole life, because if he kept off human meat when he was a wolf he turned back into a man after 9 years, though if he tasted man he stayed a wild beast for ever.'[49] When we considered the actual event which was taking place each year, the sacrifice of a human being to Zeus to propitiate and thank him for the Peloponnese, it was not difficult to understand the transformation of this reality into a somewhat murky children's story. Hyam Maccoby described such a phenomenon of transformation as a 'distancing device.'[50] It was much more comfortable for the Dorian Greeks of later centuries, such as Pausanias himself, to believe the legend rather than to know the truth. This was particularly so when describing the annual events on Mount Lykaon to children; which helped to account for the childlike logic of a man turning into a wolf for 9 years, then turning back into a man, if he hadn't eaten any human flesh in the meantime. This pattern to the legend suggested that the priest who performed the human sacrifice remained outside Dorian Greek society for 9 years in a self-accepted act of banishment for his purification.

The legend of the werewolf itself seemed to have its origination on Mount Lykaon. So the reason werewolves were terrifying figures was because they were the masks of the men who had sacrificed human beings, including children, to the supreme god. Nor was this all. Such sacrifices of propitiation and thanks to Zeus the Deliverer also carried the connotation of the extermination and absorption of the resident population, the Myceneans. Behind the façade of the legend we detected the true horror of human sacrifice and the true horror of genocide. The use of a 'distancing device' remains a universal phenomenon, Maccoby advised us; and always for the same reason. The truth is too horrific to face or to pass on to children.[51]

The sacrifice of a human life was made once a year. That was why it was 'absolutely certain' you would be dead within the year if you entered the sacrificial place. *You* would become the next sacrificial victim. The strength of the taboo against entering the place measured the horror of what took place there.

Peter Levi made this comment on the annual human sacrifice. 'Of all the observances and myths of the Greeks in this time *this is the only one by which Pausanias is really horribly shocked... the human sacrifices offered on Mount Lykaon*'[52] (my italics). It cannot be denied that human sacrifice sits ill at ease with the image of classical Greece, which Pausanias and the rest of us inherited. Pausanias himself had difficulty in facing up to this. As we have seen, when he was actually on the summit of Mount Lykaon in the sanctuary of Zeus, he said he could 'see no pleasure in pursuing enquiries' into the sacrifices.[53] But to fail to do so was to fail to understand the nature and the scale of the gratitude which the original Dorian Greek settlers felt towards Zeus for granting them the Peloponnese. Mixed in with this gratitude was god-given exemption from their guilt for the slaughter of the Myceneans.

Later on, to be sure, the human element in the sacrificial rite was dropped. So was animal sacrifice. The priests used instead 'those local honey-cakes the Athenians today [i.e. in the 2nd century AD] still call oat-meals.'[54] But propitiation and thanks continued. According to Maccoby, this pattern of dilution is also universal in foundation sacrifice.[55]

The descent down Mount Lykaon was safe. We stopped and looked back up. We had been up there in a conceivable foundation sacrifice site for ancient classical Greece. Mount Lykaon and Lycosaura are not far from Vassae, Phigalia,

Platana, Krestena, Olympia, Samikon, Kakovatos, Tegea, Mantinea, Orchomenos, and Ithome, to name only eleven outstanding Dorian Greek cities founded in the immediate vicinity of the Peloponnese. Sophia Bertram had listened and looked all day as this story unfolded. She was a grandmother knowledgeable about the history and archaeology of Greece. But she knew nothing about any of this. For me, the story ruled out Dorian Greek religion as any kind of foundation or cornerstone to our belief. This conclusion did not detract in any way from the contribution made to it by the Presocratics, Plato or Aristotle, for example. Just the opposite. It showed up, through contrast, the immensity of the achievement of the genius of the ancient Greeks, even if it also pointed up the more ancient bloody roots of the popular Dorian religion.

REFERENCES

Prologue: Paraphrase of Anselm's Proof of the Existence of God

1. Anselm, *The Major Works*, edited by Brian Davies and G. R. Evans, Oxford University Press, 1998. 'Proslogion', 'Pro Insipiente' (On Behalf of the Fool) by Gaunilo of Marmoutiers, 'Reply to Gaunilo', pp. 82-122. Anselm *(c.*1033-1109) entered the monastery at Bec in Normandy in 1059. He became Archbishop of Canterbury in 1093.
2. *The Holy Bible*, King James Version, Eyre & Spottiswoode, n.d. *The Psalms* 10:4, 14:1, 53:1-4, 73:3-9.

Chapter I: On the Aesthetics of Art in the Theology of Rowan Williams

1. Rowan Williams [henceforth RW], *Christian Imagination in Poetry and Polity: Some Anglican Voices from Temple to Herbert*, SLG Press, Convent of the Incarnation, Oxford, 2004, p. 24.
2. RW, *The Wound of Knowledge*, Darton, Longman and Todd, 1979/2004, p. 149. [Henceforth *WK*].
3. RW, *Grace and Necessity: Reflections on Art and Love*, Morehouse/Continuum Books, 2005, pp. 16-17. [Henceforth *GN*].
4. RW, *WK*, p. 1.
5. RW, *WK*, p. 152.
6. RW, *WK*, pp. 4-6.
7. RW, *WK*, p. 121.
8. RW, *WK*, p. 180.
9. RW, *WK*, p. 152.
10. RW, *WK*, p. 181.
11. RW, *GN*, p. 3.
12. RW, *GN*, p. 3.
13. RW, *GN*, p. 4.
14. RW, *GN*, p. 5.
15. RW, *GN*, pp. 8-9.
16. RW, *GN*, p. 12.
17. RW, *GN*, p. 12.
18. RW, *GN*, p. 12.
19. RW, *GN*, p. 14.
20. RW, *GN*, pp. 12-14.
21. RW, *GN*, p. 14.
22. RW, *GN*, p. 15.
23. Jacques Maritain, *Creative Intuition in Art and Poetry*, World Publishing Company/New American Library, 1954/1974, 1974 edition, p. 35; and RW, *GN*, pp. 16-17.
24. Jacques Maritain, 'Frontiers of Poetry', *Art and Scholasticism*, Sheed and Ward, 1930, p. 100, cited by RW, *GN*, p. 20.
25. RW, *GN*, p. 20.

26. RW, *GN*, pp. 18-20.
27. Jacques Maritain, 'Frontiers of Poetry', *Art and Scholasticism*, p. 101; RW, *GN*, pp. 20-21.
28. RW, *GN*, p. 21.
29. RW, *GN*, pp. 21-22.
30. Jacques Maritain, *Creative Intuition in Art and Poetry*, 'poetry has its source in the preconceptual life of the intellect', p. 3; he also calls this source 'a nonconceptual or preconceptual activity of the intellect', p. 73; and further elucidates: 'such a nonconceptual activity of the intellect, such a *nonrational activity of reason*... plays an essential part in the genesis of poetry and poetic inspiration', p. 74 (my italics); in Chapter 3, 'The Preconscious Life of the Intellect', pp. 51-74; RW, *GN*, p. 23.
31. RW, *GN*, pp. 23-24, citing Maritain, ibid., Chapter 3 and Chapter 4, 'Creative Intuition and Poetic Knowledge'.
32. RW, *GN*, p. 24.
33. RW, *GN*, p. 27.
34. RW, *GN*, p. 27.
35. RW, *GN*, p. 27.
36. RW, *GN*, pp. 27-28.
37. RW, *GN*, p. 29.
38. RW, *GN*, p. 26; see, e.g., Maritain. 'Creative Intuition and Poetic Knowledge', p. 92.
39. RW, *GN*, p. 38, in his summary of Maritain's aesthetic.
40. RW, *GN*, p. 42.
41. RW, *GN*, p. 52.
42. RW, *GN*, pp. 53-54.
43. RW, *GN*, p. 56.
44. John Keats, letter to George & Thomas Keats, 21st December 1817.
45. RW, *GN*, p. 54.
46. RW, *GN*, p. 59.
47. RW, *GN*, p. 60.
48. RW, *GN*, pp. 68-69.
49. RW, *GN*, p. 74.
50. RW, *GN*, p. 74, citing Thomas Gilby. His source is David Jones quoting Gilby in the Preface to *The Anathémata*. 'T. Gilby, in *Barbara Celarent*, writes "... the mind is a hunter of forms, *venator formarum*".'
51. RW, *GN*, p. 75.
52. RW, *GN*, p. 75.
53. RW, *GN*, p. 75.
54. RW, *GN*, p. 76.
55. RW, *GN*, p. 61.
56. RW, *GN*, p. 61.
57. RW, *GN*, p. 55.
58. RW, *GN*, pp. 76-77.
59. RW, *GN*, p. 76.
60. RW, *GN*, p. 89.
61. RW, *GN*, p. 87.
62. RW, *GN*, p. 142.
63. RW, *GN*, p. 147.
64. RW, *GN*, p. 147.
65. RW, *GN*, p. 149.
66. RW, *GN*, p. 151.
67. RW, *GN*, p. 150.
68. Martin Heidegger, *Parmenides*, translated by André Schuwer & Richard Rojcewicz, Indiana University Press, 1992, p. 3-4. His line of thought may be seen in this

passage: 'To think is to heed the essential. In such heedfulness essential knowing resides. What we usually call "knowing" is being acquainted with something and its qualities. In virtue of these cognitions we "master" things. This mastering "knowledge" is given over to a being at hand, to its structure and its usefulness. Such "knowledge" seizes the being, "dominates" it, and thereby goes beyond it and constantly surpasses it. The character of essential knowing is entirely different. It concerns the being in its ground – it intends Being. Essential "knowing" does not lord it over what it knows but is solicitous toward it. For instance, to take just one example, every "science" is a cognitive mastering, an outdoing, and a surpassing, if indeed not a complete bypassing, of a being. All of which occurs in the manner of objectivization. Versus this, *essential knowing, heedfulness, is a retreat in face of Being. In such retreating we see and perceive essentially more,* namely something quite different from the product of the remarkable procedure of modern science. For the latter is always a technical attack on a being'(my italics).

69. RW, *GN*, pp. 166-167.
70. RW, *GN*, p. 168.
71. RW, *GN*, p. 166.
72. RW, *WK*, p. 11. 'If we believe we can experience our healing without deepening our hurt, we have understood nothing of the roots of our faith.'
73. Martin Heidegger, *Being & Time* (1927), translated by John Macquarrie & Edward Robinson, Blackwell, 1993 edition, p. 62. (His italics).

Chapter II: The Moral Stance of Poetry and Its Use to Us

1. Plato, *Great Books of the Western World,* chief editor Mortimer J. Adle, volume 6, Encyclopaedia Britannica, 1952, 1993 edition, 'The Dialogues of Plato', translated by Benjamin Jowett, Book X, paragraph 608.
2. Plato, ibid., II, 379.
3. Plato, ibid., II, 379.
4. Plato, ibid., II, 379.
5. Plato, ibid., II, 379.
6. Plato, ibid., II, 380.
7. W. Montgomery Watt, *Muhammad: Prophet and Statesman,* Oxford University Press, 1961, 1967 edition, pp. 60-61.
8. W. Montgomery Watt, ibid., p. 61.
9. W. Montgomery Watt, ibid., p. 123.
10. W. Montgomery Watt, ibid., p. 123.
11. Plato, op. cit., X, 607-608.
12. Plato, ibid., X, 605-606.
13. Plato, ibid., X, 595.
14. Plato, ibid., X, 607.
15. Plato, ibid., X, 607.
16. Plato, ibid., X, 607.

Chapter III: The Roll-Over Factor

1. Lyndall Gordon, *Eliot's New Life*, Oxford University Press, 1988, p. 243.
2. *The Holy Bible*, New Revised Standard Version, HarperCollins, 1998, 'The Gospel According to John', 1:1.

Chapter IV: The Animated Dynamo

1. Henry Adams, *The Education of Henry Adams*, 100 copies privately printed 1907, first published edition 1918, this Random House edition 1931. The model is not to be confused with his 'A Dynamic Theory of History', which is Chapter 33 of the book. The model described here is best seen in Chapter 25, 'The Dynamo and the Virgin'.
2. *The Economist*, Lexington column, 'The Clinton Triangle', 4-10 November 1995.
3. George Smoot, *Wrinkles In Time*, Abacus, 1993.
4. George Smoot, ibid., p. 292.
5. George Smoot, ibid., p. 288.
6. George Smoot, ibid., pp. 278-9.
7. Stanley L. Jaki, *God and the Cosmologists*, Regnery Gateway, Washington, 1989, pp. 1-6.
8. Aristotle, *The Metaphysics*, translated by Hugh Lawson-Tancred, Penguin, 1998, 'Book Lambda 7', pp. 373-4.
9. Aristotle, *The Categories, On Interpretation, Prior Analytics*, 'The Categories', translated by Harold P. Cooke, Loeb Classical Library, Harvard University Press, 1938, 1996 edition, pp. 13-23.
10. Henry Adams, op. cit., p. 370.
11. Henry Adams, ibid., p. 370.
12. William Blake, *Complete Writings*, edited by Geoffrey Keynes, Oxford University Press, 1966, 'The Marriage of Heaven and Hell', p. 151.
13. Henry Adams, op. cit., p. 376.
14. David Jones, *Epoch and Artist*, Faber & Faber, 1959, 1973 edition, 'The Preface to *The Anathémata*', p. 113 & p. 179.
15. Henry Adams, op. cit., pp. 396-399.
16. Henry Adams, ibid., pp. 383-385.
17. Henry Adams, ibid., p. 352.
18. Henry Adams, ibid., p. 452.
19. Henry Adams, ibid., p. 382.
20. Henry Adams, ibid., p. 326.
21. Paul Davies, *About Time*, Viking, 1995, p. 279.
22. Henry Adams, op. cit., p. 385.
23. Henry Adams, ibid., p. 384.
24. Henry Adams, ibid., p. 384.
25. Henry Adams, ibid., p. 385.
26. Henry Adams, ibid., p. 384.
27. Henry Adams, ibid., p. 384.
28. Henry Adams, ibid., p. 383.
29. Henry Adams, ibid., p. 387.
30. Henry Adams, ibid., pp. 388-389.
31. Henry Adams, ibid., p. 384.
32. Henry Adams, ibid., p. 384.
33. Henry Adams, ibid., p. 385.
34. Henry Adams, ibid., p. 388.
35. Henry Adams, ibid., p. 380.
36. Henry Adams, ibid., p. 380.
37. Henry Adams, ibid., p. 383.
38. Henry Adams, ibid., p. 381.
39. Henry Adams, ibid., p. 380.
40. Henry Adams, ibid., p. 380.
41. Henry Adams, ibid., p. 380.

42.   Henry Adams, ibid., p. 381.
43.   Henry Adams, ibid., p. 383.

Chapter V: On the Resurrection of the Living and the Dead

1.   Hugh Montefiore, *On Being A Jewish Christian*, Hodder & Stoughton, 1998, pp. 93-94.
2.   Simone Weil, quoted by W. H. Auden in his introduction to *The Protestant Mystics*, edited by Anne Fremantle, New American Library, 1965, p. 15.
3.   *The Holy Bible*, containing The Old and New Testament with the Apocryphal/Deuterocanonical Books, New Revised Standard Version, Harper Collins, 1998 edition; *Isaiah* 53: 3-10. Unless otherwise stated, all citations from the bible are from this version.
4.   Hugh Montefiore, op. cit., p. 91.
5.   *Isaiah* 53:11.
6.   *The Oxford Dictionary of the Christian Church*, edited by F. L. Cross, third edition, edited by E. A. Livingstone, Oxford University Press, 1997, pp. 1016-1017.
7.   *Isaiah* 26:19.
8.   *Daniel* 12:2.
9.   *Daniel* 12:3.
10.   *New Bible Commentary*, edited by D. A. Carson *et al.*, Inter-Varsity Press, England, and Intervarsity Press, USA, 1953, 1997 edition; 'Daniel' by Sinclair B. Ferguson, p. 746.
11.   *2 Maccabees* 7:1.
12.   *2 Maccabees* 7:3.
13.   *2 Maccabees* 7:5.
14.   *2 Maccabees* 7:9.
15.   *2 Maccabees* 7:11.
16.   *2 Maccabees* 7:17.
17.   *2 Maccabees* 7:18.
18.   *2 Maccabees* 7:22-23.
19.   *2 Maccabees* 7:1.
20.   *Daniel* 12:2.
21.   *Isaiah* 66:24.
22.   *Luke* 20:36-38.
23.   *Luke* 20:40.
24.   *1 Corinthians* 15.
25.   *Oxford Dictionary of the Bible*, edited by W. R. F. Browning, Oxford University Press, 1997, p. 320.
26.   *1 Corinthians* 15:1-9.
27.   *1 Corinthians* 15:17.
28.   *1 Corinthians* 15:22.
29.   *1 Corinthians* 15:25-26.
30.   *1 Corinthians* 15:35-36.
31.   *1 Corinthians* 15:42.
32.   Hyam Maccoby, *The Sacred Executioner*, Thames & Hudson, 1982, p. 115. See also Tom Wright, *What Saint Paul Really Said*, Lion Publishing, 1997, p. 50.
33.   *1 Corinthians* 15:51-52.
34.   *The Holy Bible*, Revised Standard Version, Eyre & Spottiswoode, 1971 edition; *1 Corinthians* 15:55.
35.   *Isaiah* 66:24.

84

36. Mircea Eliade, *Shamanism: Archaic Techniques of Ecstasy*, translated from the French by Willard R. Trask, Pantheon Books, USA, 1964; Arkana/Penguin, 1989.

37. *The Epic of Gilgamesh*, an English version with an introduction by N. K. Sandars, Penguin, 1960, 1972 edition, pp. 19-20.

38. *The Epic of Gilgamesh*, ibid., p. 92.

39. *The Epic of Gilgamesh*, ibid., p. 92.

40. *The Epic of Gilgamesh*, ibid., p. 92.

41. *The Epic of Gilgamesh*, ibid., p. 97.

42. *The Epic of Gilgamesh*, ibid., p. 61.

43. *The Epic of Gilgamesh*, ibid., pp. 98, 106, 116.

44. Hyam Maccoby, op.cit., p. 116.

45. Jared Diamond, *Guns, Germs and Steel*, Jonathan Cape, 1997, Vintage edition 1998, pp. 218-222; Richard Rudgley, *Lost Civilisations of the Stone Age*, Century, 1998, p. 48.

46. *The Epic of Gilgamesh*, op. cit., p. 70.

47. *Matthew* 16:19.

48. *The Epic of Gilgamesh*, op.cit., p. 70.

49. *Matthew* 5:14.

50. *John* 8:12.

51. *The Epic of Gilgamesh*, op.cit., p. 70.

52. *Maththew* 28:18.

53. *The Epic of Gilgamesh*, op.cit., pp. 71-84.

54. *John* 16:33. Revised Standard Version.

55. *The Epic of Gilgamesh*, op.cit., p. 72.

56. *The Epic of Gilgamesh*, ibid., p. 96.

57. *Mark* 1:41.

58. *John* 11:35.

59. *The Epic of Gilgamesh*, op.cit., p. 85.

60. *The Epic of Gilgamesh*, ibid., pp. 85-87.

61. *Matthew* 4:1-11; *Mark* 1:12-13; *Luke* 4:1-13.

62. *The Epic of Gilgamesh*, op.cit., p. 92.

63. Brigitte and Gilles Delluc, *Discovering Lascaux*, translated from the French by Angela Moyon, Sud Ouest, 1990, p. 25; illustration pp. 58-59.

64. Jean-Marie Chauvet, Eliette Brunel Deschamps, and Christian Hillaire, *La Grotte Chauvet à Vallon-Pont-d'Arc*, Seuil, Paris, 1995; 'La Découverte de la Grotte Chauvet', pp. 7-80; 'La Grotte Chauvet Aujourd'hui', postface by Jean Clottes, including dating details, pp. 81-118. See also Jean Clottes and David Lewis-Williams, *Les Chamanes de la Préhistoire*, Seuil, Paris, 1996, for the link between prehistoric cave painting and shamanism.

65. Henry de Lumley, *Time: The Weekly Newsmagazine*, vol.145 no.6, February 13, 1995, quoted by Robert Hughes, cover story, 'Behold the Stone Age', pp. 32-39.

66. See, for example, C. G. Jung, *Symbols of Transformation*, translated by R. F. C. Hull, Routledge & Kegan Paul, 1956, second edition, 1967, plate XIX. This example dates from 885-860 BC, the palace of Assurnasirpal II, Nimrud, Assyria.

67. *John* 6:48.

68. *John* 11:25-26.

69. *Ezekiel* 1:28.

70. *The Epic of Gilgamesh*, op.cit., p. 92.

71. *The Epic of Gilgamesh*, ibid., p. 92.

72. *Matthew* 16:21-23; 17:22-23; 20:17-19. *Mark* 8:31-33; 9:30-32; 10:32-34. *Luke* 9:21-22; 9:43-45; 18:31-34.

73. *Matthew* 11:28-30.

74. *Matthew* 5:4.

75.   *The Epic of Gilgamesh*, op.cit., p. 97.
76.   *The Epic of Gilgamesh*, ibid., p. 113. Like Noah after him, Utnapishtim took his household on board the ark. What happened to his children and craftsmen is left unclear, but his unnamed wife is stated as enjoying 'everlasting life' with him: pp. 107, 113, 114.
77.   *The Epic of Gilgamesh*, ibid, pp. 97, 121.
78.   *Matthew* 4:4. *Deuteronomy* 8:3.
79.   *The Epic of Gilgamesh*, op.cit., pp. 97-107.
80.   *Matthew* 26: 36-46. *Mark* 14:32-42. *Luke* 22:39-46.
81.   *Matthew* 27:27-54. *Mark* 15:16-39. *Luke* 23:26-49. *John* 19:16-30.
82.   *The Epic of Gilgamesh*, op.cit., pp. 102-103, 105.
83.   *The Epic of Gilgamesh*, ibid., introduction by N. K. Sandars, pp. 39-40.
84.   Maimonides, *The Commandments: Sefer Ha-Mitzvoth of Maimonides*, 2 vols., translated from the Hebrew by Charles B. Chavel, Soncino Press, 1967, 1990 edition, 'The Thirteen Basic Principles of Faith: Resurrection', vol.1, p. 280.
85.   Philip Birnbaum, *Encyclopedia of Jewish Concepts*, Hebrew Publishing Company, New York, 1964, 1993 edition, p. 630.
86.   *Luke* 22:42.
87.   *Luke* 22:46.
88.   *The Epic of Gilgamesh*, op.cit., p. 108.
89.   *The Epic of Gilgamesh*, ibid., p. 108.
90.   *John* 12:47.
91.   *John* 4:22.
92.   *John* 4:25-26.
93.   *The Epic of Gilgamesh*, op.cit., pp. 111-112.
94.   *Genesis* 8:21. *The Epic of Gilgamesh*, ibid., p. 111.
95.   *Hebrews* 7:26-28
96.   *Matthew* 26:26-28.
97.   *John* 6:53-58.
98.   *John* 3:16.
99.   *The Epic of Gilgamesh*, op.cit., p. 114.
100. *The Epic of Gilgamesh*, ibid., p. 105.
101. *The Epic of Gilgamesh*, ibid., p. 114.
102. *The Epic of Gilgamesh*, ibid., pp. 114-115.
103. *Luke* 22:44.
104. *Matthew* 27:46.
105. *The Psalms* 22:1; 10:1.
106. *The Epic of Gilgamesh*, op.cit., p. 115.
107. *The Epic of Gilgamesh*, ibid., p. 116.
108. *The Epic of Gilgamesh*, ibid., p. 117.
109. *Genesis* 2:9; 3:22.
110. *The Epic of Gilgamesh*, op.cit., pp. 118-119.
111. *Romans* 6:23.
112. *The Epic of Gilgamesh*, op.cit., p. 119.
113. *The Epic of Gilgamesh*, ibid., p. 119.
114. *The Epic of Gilgamesh*, ibid., p. 119.
115. *Genesis* 14:17-20.
116. *The Epic of Gilgamesh*, op.cit., p. 118.
117. *Genesis* 14:13-20.
118. *The Epic of Gilgamesh*, op.cit., pp. 118-119.
119. Hyam Maccoby, op. cit., pp. 116-117
120. *The Epic of Gilgamesh*, op.cit., introduction by N. K. Sandars, pp. 7-13.
121. *Luke* 22:19.

122. *John* 14:6.
123. *John* 11:25.
124. *John* 19:17.
125. *The Tibetan Book of the Dead*, edited by W. Y. Evans-Wentz, Oxford University Press, 1927, 1968 edition, p. lix. Dating of the text, p. 73.
126. *The Tibetan Book of the Dead*, op.cit., pp. xvi-xvii.

Chapter VI: The Foundation Sacrifice of the Dorian Greek Nation

1. *The Oxford History of the Classical World*, edited by John Boardman, Jasper Griffin, and Oswyn Murray, Guild Publishing/Book Club Associates/Oxford University Press, 1986, p. 830.
2. J. P. Mallory, *In Search of the Indo-Europeans,* Thames and Hudson, 1989, 1992 edition, pp. 66-71. The conjectured non-Indo-European nature of the Mycenean language is a subject of controversy. When Michael Ventris deciphered its Linear B script in terms of an early form of Greek in 1952 the controversy intensified. See, for example, Semni Karouzou, *National Museum* [of Greece]: *Illustrated Guide to the Museum*, Ekdotike Athenon S.A., Athens, 1977, 1994 edition, pp. 21-22 and p. 36; A. R. Burn, *The Pelican History of Greece*, Penguin, 1966, 1979 edition, p. 42; George E. Mylonas, *Mycenae: A Guide to its Ruins and its History*, Ekdotike Athenon S. A., Athens, 1981, 1987 edition, p. 94.
3. *The Oxford History of the Classical World*, op.cit., 'Introduction' by Jasper Griffin, p. 4
4. George E. Mylonas, *Mycenae: A Guide to its Ruins and its History*, op.cit., p. 87.
5. *The Oxford History of the Classical World*, op.cit., p. 837.
6. *The Oxford History of the Classical World*, ibid., 'Greece: The History of the Archaic Period' by George Forrest, p. 20.
7. A. R. Burn, *The Pelican History of Greece*, op.cit., p. 31.
8. *The Oxford History of the Classical World*, op.cit., 'Introduction' by Jasper Griffin, p. 4.
9. *The Oxford History of the Classical World*, ibid., pp. 4-5.
10. John Cuthbert Lawson, *Modern Greek Folklore and Ancient Greek Religion: A Study in Survivals*, first edition 1909, University Books, New York, 1964, pp. 522-523; Pausanias, *Guide to Greece*, 2 vols., translated and edited by Peter Levi, vol. 2, 'Southern Greece', Penguin, 1971, p. 371.
11. Pausanias, *Guide to Greece, ibid.*
12. *The Oxford Classical Dictionary*, edited by N. G. L. Hammond and H. H. Scullard, Oxford Dictionary Press, 1970, 1973 edition, p. 793.
13. Pausanias, *Guide to Greece*, op. cit., pp. 370-371.
14. Pausanias, ibid., p. 371.
15. Pausanias, ibid., p. 371.
16. Pausanias, ibid., p. 373.
17. Pausanias, ibid., p. 376.
18. A. R. Burn, *The Pelican History of Greece*, op.cit., p. 30.
19. A. R. Burn, ibid., p. 30.
20. Pausanias, ibid., *Guide to Greece*, op.cit., p. 371.
21. Pausanias, ibid., p. 466.
22. *The Times Atlas of the Bible*, edited by James B. Pritchard, Times Books, 1987, p. 26.
23. *The Epic of Gilgamesh*, edited by N. K. Sandars, Penguin, 1960, 1972 edition, p. 20 and p. 117.
24. Pausanias, *Guide to Greece*, op.cit., footnote by Peter Levi, pp. 174-175.

25. Herodotus, *The Histories*, translated by Aubrey de Sélincourt, Penguin, 1954, 1968 edition, p. 85.
26. Pausanias, *Guide to Greece*, op.cit., p. 376.
27. Pausanias, ibid., p. 466.
28. Hyam Maccoby, *The Sacred Executioner*, Thames and Hudson, 1982, pp. 27-28, 97, 179-180, 187.
29. *Deuteronomy* 12:2; 2 *Kings* 16:4; *Isaiah* 57:5; *Jeremiah* 2:20; *Ezekiel* 6:13; *Hosea* 4:13.
30. *Genesis* 22: 1-19.
31. Pausanias, *Guide to Greece*, op.cit., p. 466. See also Robert Graves, *The Greek Myths*, Penguin, 1955; The Folio Society, 2 vols., 1999, p. 46. '[Rhea] bore Zeus, her third son, at dead of night on Mount Lykaon in Arcadia.'
32. Pausanias, ibid., p. 371.
33. Pausanias, ibid., p. 371.
34. Pausanias, ibid., p. 467.
35. Pausanias, ibid., p. 468.
36. Pausanias, ibid., p. 468.
37. Robert Graves, *The Greek Myths*, op.cit., p. 214; *Pears Cyclopaedia*, 66th edition, A. & F. Pears, 1957-1958, 'Greek Myths and Legends', p. 680.
38. Pausanias, op.cit., pp. 468-469.
39. Pausanias, ibid., footnote by Peter Levi, p. 468.
40. Pausanias, ibid., footnote by Peter Levi, p. 468. See also John Cuthbert Lawson, *Modern Greek Folklore and Ancient Greek Religion*, op.cit., pp. 352-353.
41. Hyam Maccoby, op.cit., pp. 27-28, 97, 179-180, 187.
42. Pausanias, op.cit., p. 466.
43. Pausanias, ibid., p. 466.
44. Pausanias, ibid., p. 371.
45. Pausanias, ibid., p. 372.
46. *The Compact Edition of the Oxford English Dictionary*, 2 vols., Oxford University Press, 1971, 1976 edition, p. 1683.
47. Pausanias, op.cit., p. 372.
48. Pausanias, ibid., p. 372.
49. Pausanias, ibid., p. 373.
50. Hyam Maccoby, op.cit., pp. 50, 97.
51. Hyam Maccoby, ibid., pp. 50, 97.
52. Pausanias, op.cit., footnote by Peter Levi, p. 372.
53. Pausanias, ibid., pp. 468-469.
54. Pausanias, ibid., p. 372.
55. Hyam Maccoby, op.cit., pp. 27-28, 97, 179-180, 187.

This book is the first part

of a two volume work.

The second part is titled

The Wheels of Ezekiel:

A Theology of Poetry (Mellen, 2009).